Shore diving near Seattle

Alexander Wallner
Maxwell Wallner
Kent Wallner

SmartMedicine Press
Seattle, Washington

First Edition

ISBN 13: 978-0-9648991-7-9

Published by SmartMedicine Press, Seattle, Washington
Cover design by Deborah Rust, New York, New York
Distributed by Pathway Book Service, Gilsum, NH 800-345-6665

dedicated to

Kathryn Elliott
mother, wife, physician, scientist and attorney

Acknowledgments

The following people helped us in our journey to write this book. Their insightful comments, suggestions and encouragement were invaluable:

Christofer Borg, CMD
Paul Herstein, MD
Bruce Higgins
Kimberle Stark

Pat Jewell, MD
Colleen Simpson, RN
James Trask
Joe Weiss

Important caution #1

This book is intended to educate Puget Sound divers and to enhance safety through knowledge. The content is in no way intended to replace formal dive instruction. All divers should have completed certified dive instruction and should keep their skills up-to-date in it.

Important caution #2

Our descriptions of the dive sites in this book are current as of November, 2008. It is *certain* that government agencies, private organizations or rogue individuals will alter some sites for commercial, environmental or recreational purposes. Before diving a site, it is imperative that you seek information disseminated after publication of this book. Sources of newer information include posted signs at the site, more recent dive books, experts at your local dive shop, and internet searches.

Important caution #3

We show approximate depths (in feet) in many of the figures as a matter of interest and to help divers anticipate where structures should be found. The numbers are usually given as a 10-foot range, to allow for tidal differences (see chapter *Tides and currents*). These depths should be viewed strictly as approximations. They can differ from reality by as much as 5-10 feet, depending on wind conditions and where precisely you position your depth gauge.

Your input

We had a good time researching and writing this book. So much so that we started planning a second edition before the ink was dry on this one. Any suggestions or corrections that you might have are welcome. We especially would like to acknowledge divers and others who have worked to make our dive sites what they are. For instance: *Who made the underwater fish sculpture at Les Davis?*

ShoreDivingComments@gmail.com

Contents

Why this book?

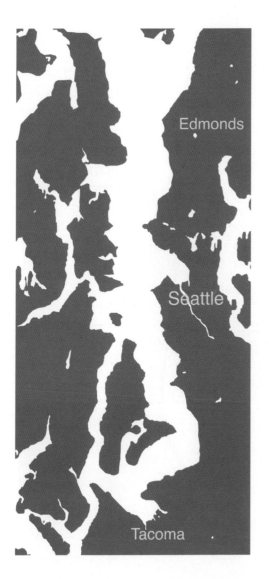

The Pacific Northwest is a great place to live and dive. We're socially progressive. We work in cutting edge information, manufacturing and medical industries. For recreation, we can choose between spectacular mountains and an equally spectacular ocean, right at our doorstep (**Figure 1**).

A growing sport

Scuba diving is a growing sport. Approximately 2,000 new divers are certified each year in the Puget Sound area. Diving opens up a fascinating new world. Witnessing the diversity of marine life and ex-

Cascade Mountains

Figure 1. The beauty of our oceans rivals that of our mountains. It just takes more equipment and training to explore the ocean.

Titlow Marine Preserve

ploring the structure of the world underwater is a remarkable adventure.

Shore diving

When most people think of scuba diving, they think of *boat* dives—a fully-geared diver rolling backward off the side of a boat into warm tropical waters. This book is about something different. *Shore-diving* refers to gearing up at the beach, walking down to the water, and wading in (**Figure 2**). Compared to boat diving, shore diving is simple, quick, and cheap (**Figure 3**).

There are over 100 public shore-dive sites around the Sound, readily accessible to anyone with gear and a car to transport it. Most sites are at *free* public parks—you need only bring enough money to pay for a celebratory meal afterwards.

Why this dive guide was written

When we took up diving, we had no idea that two years later we would be writing this book. There are a lot of other things we should be doing instead. But we *are* writing this, and the reason is simple: we would have loved to have a book like this when we began our scuba forays into the challenging waters of Puget Sound.

Without a detailed guide book, you'd learn about dive sites by talking with other divers and searching the internet. You might go with a friend or professional guide. While these other sources can be invaluable, we found ourselves going to new sites without a guide, feeling unprepared as to where to park, where to enter the water, and where to go once we were underwater. We had to visit some sites several times to see the highlights of those sites. We could easily have gotten discouraged, especially in our first few trips. We kept pushing on, but realized that others may not be as willing to push through the early get-acquainted stages. That would be a shame. We don't want *you* to get discouraged before you appreciate the thrill of shore-diving the Sound.

Where we will take you

With over 100 dive sites around the Sound, how do you decide where to start? The easiest way is to visit the ones that have proven most popular with other divers. The eleven sites described here are rela-

Shore-diving 101

step 1
load gear

step 2
drive to beach

step 3
gear up

step 4
walk into water

Figure 2. Shore-diving refers to gearing up at the beach, walking down to the water, and wading in. It's cheaper, quicker and easier than boat-diving.

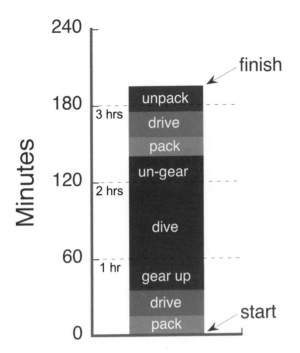

Figure 3. Urban shore dives do not necesarily take a long time. We are generally door-to-door in about three hours.

tively easy to get to, relatively safe, and interesting to explore (**Figure 4**). They are solid places to sip the joys and thrills of cold-water shore-diving.

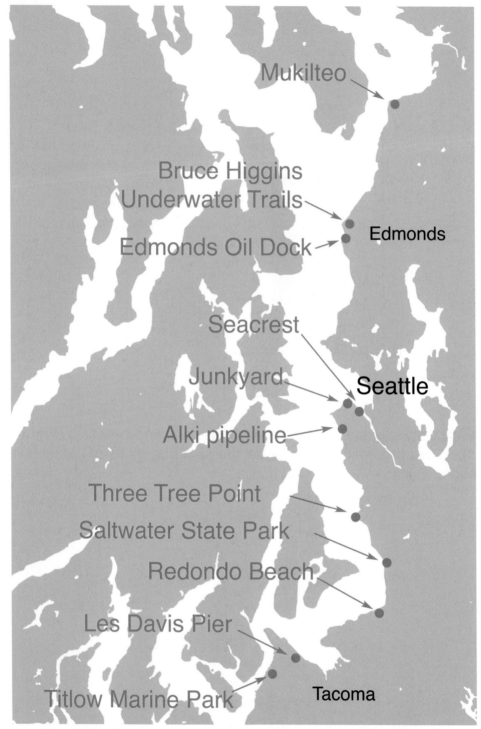

Figure 4. These are the eleven most popular dive sites in the Seattle-Edmonds-Tacoma region.

Tacoma

Bruce Higgins Underwater Trails

Figure 5. Old-fashioned pollution. This is relatively easy to identify, and we know how to fix it.

Save the Sound

We *want* you to dive Puget Sound. Partly because we are scuba-crazy, and want to share our infatuation with you. But also because the more people dive the Sound, the more they will be committed to preserving it. The old sources of pollution have largely been addressed (**Figure 5**). While litter and factory pollution can be identified and dealt with directly, the Sound has always faced broader issues of habitat losses and more diffuse pollution sources that all of us contribute to: our cars, our lawns, even the medications that we contribute to the waste stream. Today, these threats continue from ongoing population growth and are exacerbated by climate change.

The population from Hood Canal to the Canadian border is projected to grow from approximately 4 million in 2000 to 5.5 million by 2025 (**Figure 6**). Protecting our waters and the life they hold will require tough personal and political choices. These choices often mean spending public and personal dollars. Witnessing the rich but fragile marine life just off our shores will galvanize more of us to support bet-

Figure 6. Insidious pollution sources from population growth are not so obvious. Counteracting their effects requires expensive, politically difficult choices.

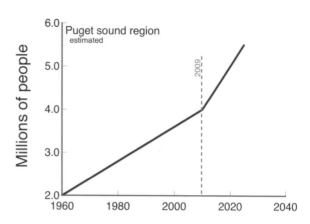

ter ecological choices in our daily lives and in our political activities and decisions.

Divers, perhaps more than anyone, experience and appreciate the beauty that the Sound holds. Divers see the usually unseen treasure at risk if we do not tend to our water's health. We hope that this book inspires you to become an avid cold-water diver and a passionate Sound advocate. The more you dive, the more you will care about the Sound, its health and its future.

Quickies

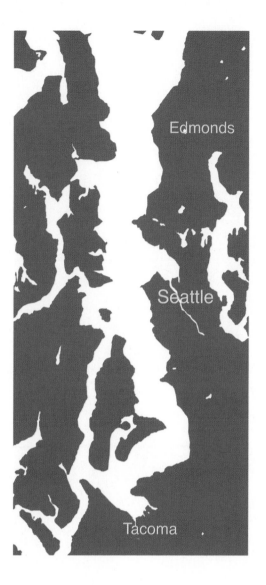

This book presents a fairly detailed summary of eleven popular dive sites within a 30 minute drive of downtown Seattle. But you're in a hurry? The next five pages is the very abridged version. You might make a quick choice from our thumbnail sketch, but take time to look through the site's full chapter before submerging.

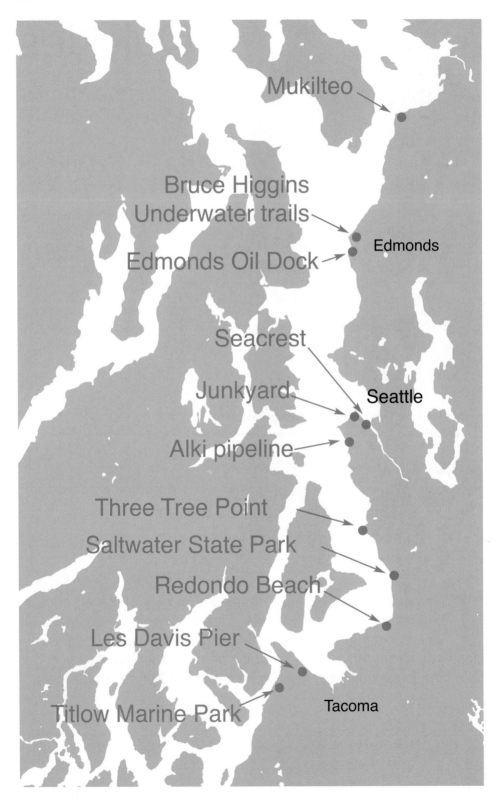

Mukilteo

Bruce Higgins
Underwater trails

Edmonds Oil Dock

Edmonds

Seacrest

Junkyard

Seattle

Alki pipeline

Three Tree Point

Saltwater State Park

Redondo Beach

Les Davis Pier

Titlow Marine Park

Tacoma

Three Tree Point

Pros
  some interesting reef structure
Cons
  limited marine life

Bruce Higgins Underwater Trails

Pros
  incredible reef structure
  lots of marine life
  good car access
  shower
Cons
  crowded at times
  viz can be inferior

Edmonds Marina Beach

Pros
  good car access
  lots of marine life
Cons
  intense currents

The Junkyard at Alki

Pros
  interesting structure
  fair amount of marine life
  easy to navigate
  good car access
Cons
  junky

Les Davis
Marine Park

Pros
  interesting structure
  good car access
  easy to navigate
Cons
  suboptimal viz

Mukilteo Community
Beach

Pros
  good car access
  some interesting structure
Cons
  limited marine life
  over-dived

Alki Pipeline

Pros

good car access
interesting structure.
lots of marine life

Cons

long swim
tricky to navigate

Redondo Beach

Pros

amusing structure
easy to navigate
good car access
shower

Cons

junky
over-dived

Saltwater State Park

Pros

interesting structure
lots of marine life
good car access
shower

Cons

long swim

Seacrest

Pros
some interesting structure
good car access
shower
Cons
often crowded
limited marine life

Titlow Marine Park

Pros
interesting structure
lots of marine life
easy to navigate
good car access
shower
Cons
STRONG CURRENTS

Gear

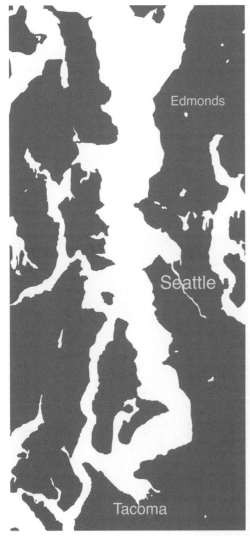

Edmonds

Seattle

Tacoma

B y the time you're scuba-certified, you'll be familiar with the basic gear needed to dive the cold waters of Puget Sound. We won't waste much space here describing what is in any basic scuba manual. However, we have figured out a few ways to make gear management a little easier. We'd like to share with you a few lessons that we learned the hard way.

Extras

Besides your basic scuba gear, a few additional items are helpful. All of the dive sites described here were once (or still are) fishing

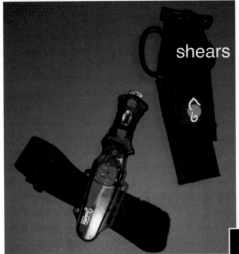

shears *Figure 1. Most divers carry a cutting tool (or two).*

Figure 2. Underwater writing slates can make for a more efficient dive experience, especially at sites that are new to you or your buddy.

Figure 3. Flashlights are available in a variety of sizes, strengths and cost ($20 and way up).

spots. Lost fishing line is a hazard to wildlife and to divers. Getting tangled in old line is a scuba nightmare. Considering how difficult it can be to see fishing line, let alone untangle yourself from it, most divers carry a knife or shears (**Figure 1**).

Underwater communication can come in handy, and basic scuba hand language is often not enough. A variety of underwater writing slates are available (**Figure 2**). A pencil is used to write on a rough plastic board. The writing is erasable with sand. Slates can save you and your buddy a trip to the surface to discuss issues about your dive (what direction to go, what weird fish just swam by, etc.).

One of the highlights of Puget Sound diving is exploring rock crevices and reef dens for octopi, eels or almost anything else that likes to hide. Flashlights are good for exploring for hidden life. They also can bring out color at deeper sites—it can get pretty dark in poor visibility (viz) or on cloudy days (**Figure 3**).

One of the potential dangers of shore diving in the high tidal exchanges of Puget Sound is finding yourself too far from shore to get back on your own. Any combination of fatigue, physical problems, navigation errors or nasty currents could get you too far from shore. There are a variety of signalling devices, including whistles and bright-colored floats that strap to your buoyancy control device (BCD) (**Figure 4**). Carrying one or more of these safety devices is a good idea. The longer it takes them to find you, the bigger that Coast Guard bill may be.

Most divers enter the water each time wearing hundreds or thousands of dollars of gear. Assuming that you want to leave the water with all of the expensive gear you started with, *everything* should be attached to you somehow. Lanyards are good. Retractable lines are good (**Figure 5**). Searching for a lost camera or expensive flashlight almost always ends in disappointment.

Organizing gear at home
It helps to keep all of of your gear organized in one spot, where you can check it and keep it organized between dives (**Figure 6**). If your gear is organized well, packing for a dive can be done in less than 10 minutes.

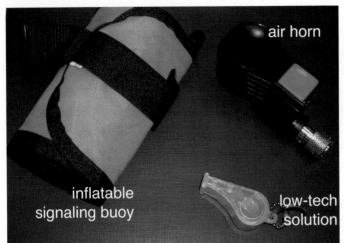

Figure 4. A variety of increasingly sophisticated signaling devices is available.

air horn

inflatable
signaling buoy

low-tech
solution

Figure 5. Use fasteners to attach your gadgets to yourself or your BCD.

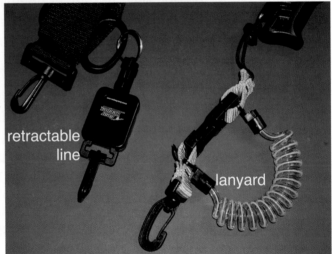

retractable
line

lanyard

Checklist

When it comes to cold water diving, forgetting almost anything will make your dive more dangerous, uncomfortable, or both. Despite having been on hundreds of Puget Sound dives, we still go through a checklist just before leaving the house (**Figure 7**). Doing so can save you the heartbreak of loading your car, driving 25 minutes to the site, and realizing that you forgot a glove.

Gearing up

If you are new to shore diving, you will quickly see that there are many ways to gear-up at the site. Most divers do so at their car and walk to the water fully geared (**Figures 8 and 9**). In nice weather, we like the leisure of gearing up on the the beach (**Figure 10**). Your options will be dictated largely by your type of vehicle and available parking.

Valuables

Car break-ins are a reality at outdoor recreation spots. It's a problem at hiking trailheads around the state, and scuba trailheads carry the same risk. You may be leaving your car unattended at a spot where thieves can be fairly confident that you won't be around for an hour or so.

While we always consider the possibility of thievery, we have not had trouble ourselves, or even heard first hand of such a problem. But be realistic and be careful. One solution is to bring a non-diver friend (canine or human) to car sit. But that's usually not practical.

Minimize the valuables you leave in your car, and keep your car keys with you on your dive (**Figure 12**). And make it as obvious as possible that there is nothing worth taking. Don't leave exposed packages that tempt potential thieves.

Washing up

Rinse the saltwater from your gear as soon as possible after each dive (**Figure 13**). Some of the sites described here have working showers on site from spring through fall. Nearby dive shops usually have a fresh water rinse station. In the absence of a more convenient situation, we use a tub and a hanger outside our garage.

Figure 6. Our home scuba head-quarters.

Figure 7. A checklist can save you from that arrive-at-site-missing-stuff heartbreak. Organize your gear in plastic boxes to help avoid forgetting something, and to protect your car from saltwater damage.

bungy cords keep tanks from falling

Figure 8. Most shore divers gear up at their cars.

Figure 9. These divers are making a pretty long walk from a parking lot to the beach at Redondo.

Figure 10. We like to gear up near the water's edge, depending on the parking situation. This convenient cement wall is just up from the beach at the Alki Pipeline. The driftwood-strewn beach on the right is at Saltwater State Park.

keys hooked to BCD

waterproof box

*Figure 12. Try to not to leave valu-
ables in your car. There are simple
ways to take smaller valuables with
you on your dive.*

Saltwater State Park

dive shop

*Figure 13. Find a way to
rinse your gear soon after
your dive.*

back alley

Seasons

The surface temperature of Puget Sound stays between 40-48°F year round. At 40 feet or deeper, the temperature is pretty steady at 46°F. Anything less than 60°F is very cold to humans, and requires a wetsuit or drysuit. Diving here any time of the year is referred to as *cold water diving*.

Although the water is cold year-round, there are big seasonal differences in typical weather conditions, including air temperature, rainfall and cloudiness (**Figure 1**). These weather conditions affect divers in

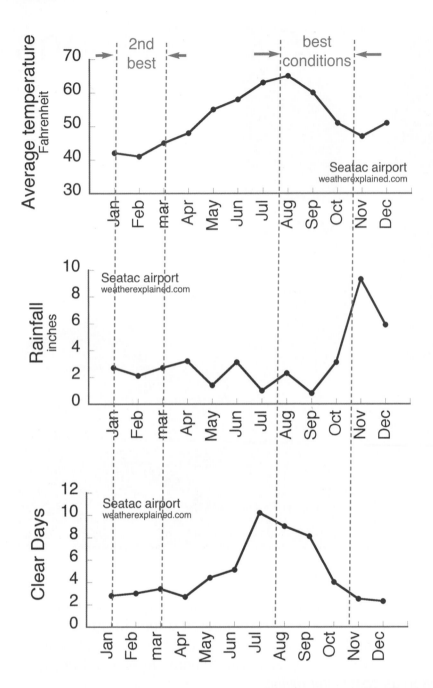

Figure 1. *Ambient weather conditions vary markedly during the year. In general, the best mix of visibility and out-of-water comfort are from August through October. But you can get great or not-so-great dive conditions on any given day all year round.*

February
36°F

hardcore divers

heated tent

August
68°F

two ways: visibility and out-of-water comfort. Hard-core divers care far more about the former than the latter.

There is little question that fall diving (August through October) offers the best dive conditions above *and* below the surface. The plankton bloom has subsided and there are plenty of sunny days to give more light at depth. And it's usually warm enough to make changing into and out of your gear a fairly comfortable experience.

The winter months of January through March typically provide the second best dive conditions. The biggest problem with winter diving is changing into and out of gear in a cold rain—not high on most people's fun-things-to-do list. However, because of the typically good viz during the winter, you will see plenty of other divers. Tents, rain flys, etc. can soften the discomfort of gear-changing in unpleasant weather conditions (**Figure 2**).

Unfortunately, spring and summer typically offer the worst visibility conditions. We still go during those months, but sparingly. If you can't wait till August, try checking the viz beforehand for a not-so-bad day (see Chapter 7).

Tides
and
currents

P ay attention. This is the most important chapter in this book. Tides in Puget Sound produce some of the largest water level changes and strongest ocean currents in North America. Currents that result from tidal forces have a dramatic effect on dive conditions. Diving in strong currents is tiring and can be downright dangerous. While we love diving Puget Sound, the hazards posed by its highly variable currents are real. Even if you have no interest whatsoever in the science of tidal flows, you must appreciate the power of the tides and you should have at least a simple understanding of how to plan dives at relatively safe tidal times.

Figure 1. Relationship of earth, moon and tidal force. Due to its proximity to the earth, the moon exerts twice as much tidal force than does the sun.

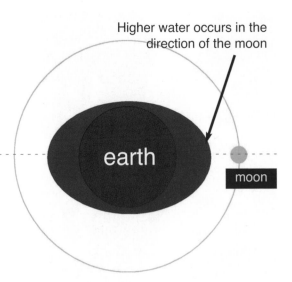

Higher water occurs in the direction of the moon

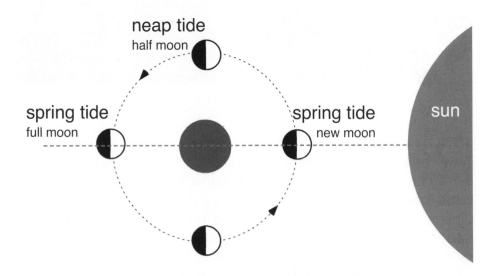

Figure 2. Spring (maximum) tides occur when the moon and sun are aligned.

Tides 101

Tides are caused by the gravitational pull of the moon and the sun on the oceans (**Figure 1**). There are two high and two low tides each day. The tides occur about one hour later each successive day. Tidal heights vary in 30 day cycles, depending largely on the alignment of the earth, moon and sun. Higher *spring* tides occur when the moon and earth are aligned with the sun (**Figure 2**). *Neap* tides are lower.

The two high tides that occur each day are of different heights (**Figure 3**). The same is true for the two low tides. The magnitude of the disparity in tidal heights on a given day is related to the angle of the moon's orbit to the earth's equator. The difference in consecutive high and low tidal heights is referred to as the *tidal exchange*.

The tidal range on the open ocean is about 2.5 feet. However, the range in Puget Sound is 10-12 feet, due to shoreline effects on water movement. Changing tidal heights can make a substantial difference in the shore view of a dive site (**Figure 4**).

Published water depths and tidal heights are based on measurements taken by NOAA—the National Oceanographic and Atmospheric Administration. On nautical charts, the water's depth is described in MLLW—the mean lower low water depth. To calculate the depth at a given time, add the tidal height from a tide almanac to the stated depth on your nautical map (**Figure 5**). During neap tides, the water's depth will be slightly lower than the MLLW. These extremely low water intervals are the best times for non-divers to explore tide pools. In this book, the approximate depth is given in many of the figures. It is always given as a 10-foot range, to allow for tidal differences. These depths should be viewed as approximations; they may differ from reality by a few feet depending on wind conditions.

Despite relatively large water level changes with the tides, most divers make little effort to plan dives around the tidal heights. With most marine life and structure found between 20-70 feet depth, a 10 foot tidal difference won't affect where you can go and what you can see. However, the tidal height can influence visibility. At lower tidal heights, if all else is the same, you will get more sunlight on the ocean floor because the light travels through less water. However, despite better sunlight with lower tidal height, higher tidal heights may actually pro-

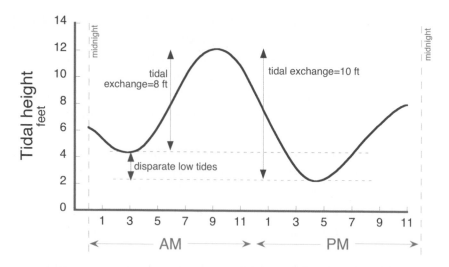

Figure 3. *The two high tide and low tide points each day are of different heights. Tidal exchanges vary markedly, depending on the phase of the moon. They range from 2 to 12 feet. Currents are stronger during times of higher tidal exchanges.*

Figure 4. *Beach view of Titlow Marine Preserve dive site at high versus low tide. Low tide makes for a longer walk from the gear-up area to the water's edge.*

duce better viz because there is less plankton at deeper depths. This balance between sunlight and visibility at depth changes from day to day.

Currents 101

Ocean currents result from a complex interaction between tidal pulls, water temperatures and surface wind. Changing tidal heights are the dominant force driving water currents within the sound. Currents are stronger when the tidal exchange is larger (**Figure 3**). While tidal heights may not have much impact on your dive, the currents generated by tidal exchanges will.

Flood refers to the time when water flows into the sound, toward the shore. *Maximum flood* refers to the time of fastest current. *Slack* is the 30-60 minutes of minimal water speed, when the tidal flow changes direction. The faster the maximum current at a particular site, the shorter the slack time will be (**Figure 6**). Keep in mind that slack times are not accurate to the minute. They can vary due to weather conditions.

Current speeds vary markedly around Puget Sound, being strongest in places where the sound is narrowest (**Figure 7**). NOAA maintains seven current monitors that are submerged in deep water around Puget Sound. The Admiralty Inlet station covers all dive sites described in this book except for Titlow and Les Davis. They are monitored by The Narrows current station. Measurements taken at the current stations are the basis for current time predictions in published tide guides (see below). Be careful—using current station data to predict shoreline currents is somewhat inaccurate due to water flow differences between deep water and the shoreline.

The most dangerous currents for the dives described here are at Titlow Marine Preserve in the Tacoma Narrows, where a lot of water has to pass through a relatively narrow channel. Current speeds exceed 4 knots, as opposed to typical maximum of 1 or 2 knots at sites like Edmonds, Alki and Three Tree. Currents tend to be weaker at sites where the shoreline protrudes into the Sound (*headlands*). Headlands cause back eddy currents that tend to be weaker and in the direction opposite to the main water flow. The strength and direction of eddy currents are difficult to predict accurately.

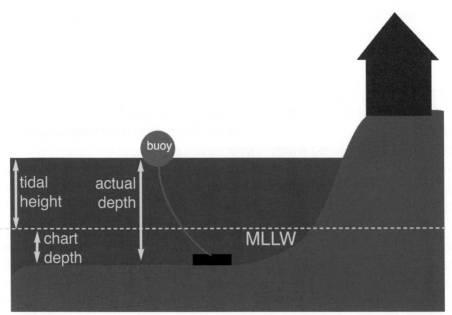

Figure 5. MLLW is the average depth at low tide. It is the con-
ventional way to describe water depth on nautical charts. The
actual water depth at any given time is the MLLW plus the tidal
height at that time.

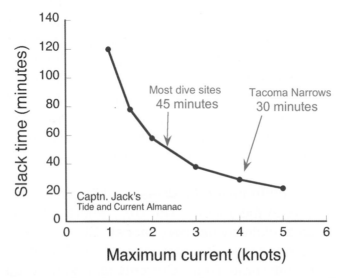

Figure 6. The faster the maximum current at a dive site, the
shorter will be the slack interval. Consider these times to be
estimates only, as they are subject to weather, lunar, and sun
conditions.

While we don't pay much heed to tidal heights when planning our dives, we *do* pay attention to currents. They can be quite strong and potentially dangerous, depending on where and when you dive (see Chapter 9). Current tables can be used to plan your dive around the slack times. Even if you don't let currents dictate when you dive, it is a good idea to be aware of the approximate current strength and direction that you will face down below.

Tidal almanacs

Tidal almanacs give detailed tidal and current times, and can be purchased for a few dollars, depending on their level of detail and readability (**Figure 8**). Considering the effect that tides and currents have on dive conditions, all divers should have one (or more). The easiest to use almanacs show graphical representations of the tidal height for each day of the year (**Figures 9-12**). If you are new to tidal charts, make sure to read the directions so that you understand what you're looking at. Most importantly, you need to appreciate that there is a disconnect between the tidal heights and current strength, with maximum flow and slack times typically occurring an hour or more after their respective low or high tides (**Figures 10 and 11**).

Being practical

While the current does not have to dictate your dive times at most sites described here, the safest policy is to plan your dives to be as close as possible to slack times.

Some divers will dive in moderate currents. Maybe because it is not always possible to mesh optimal current times with a busy work life. Other divers simply don't check their tidal almanac beforehand. If you choose to dive in currents, you must be careful to start your dive going against or across the current, and return to shore with the current (**Figure 13**). This is important! Trying to return to shore against a current is a big-time scuba no-no (see Chapter 9).

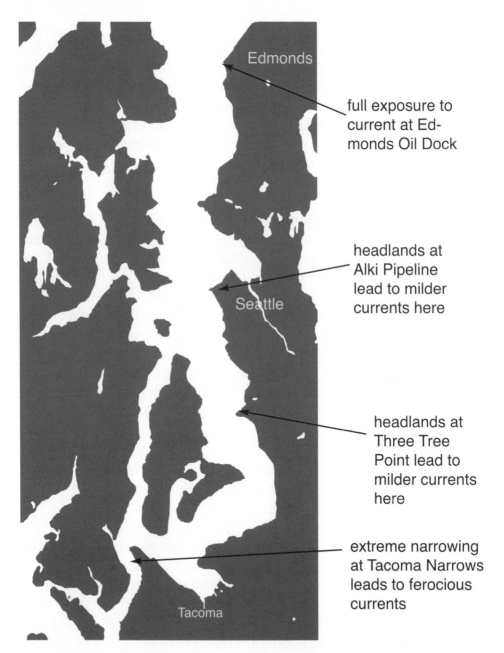

full exposure to current at Edmonds Oil Dock

headlands at Alki Pipeline lead to milder currents here

headlands at Three Tree Point lead to milder currents here

extreme narrowing at Tacoma Narrows leads to ferocious currents

Figure 7. The shape of the coast line has a large influence on the currents at a dive site. At sites where land juts out into the sound the currents will generally be weaker, but less predictable.

Figure 8. There is a variety of inexpensive tide and current guides. Get one or more for your dive planning. There are also several online tidal guides.

water level above MLLW

Figure 9. This page from the Tidelog shows the tides and currents for four consecutive days.

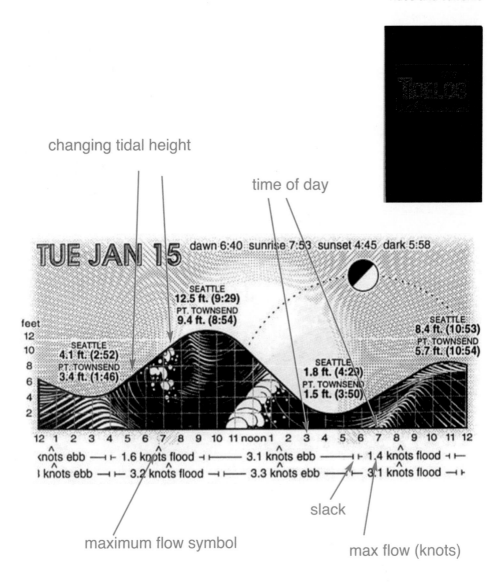

changing tidal height

time of day

TUE JAN 15   dawn 6:40 sunrise 7:53 sunset 4:45 dark 5:58

SEATTLE
12.5 ft. (9:29)
PT. TOWNSEND
9.4 ft. (8:54)

SEATTLE
4.1 ft. (2:52)
PT. TOWNSEND
3.4 ft. (1:46)

SEATTLE
1.8 ft. (4:23)
PT. TOWNSEND
1.5 ft. (3:50)

SEATTLE
8.4 ft. (10:53)
PT. TOWNSEND
5.7 ft. (10:54)

feet
12
10
8
6
4
2

12 1 2 3 4 5 6 7 8 9 10 11 noon 1 2 3 4 5 6 7 8 9 10 11 12

‹nots ebb —ɪ ⊢ 1.6 knots flood ⊣ ⊢——— 3.1 knots ebb ———ɪ ⊢ 1.4 knots flood ⊣ ⊢—
) knots ebb —ɪ ⊢ 3.2 knots flood —ɪ ⊢—— 3.3 knots ebb ———ɪ⊢ 3.1 knots flood —ɪ ⊢

slack

maximum flow symbol

max flow (knots)

Figure 10. This blow-up of a tidal chart from Tidelog shows the tidal heights throughout the day. The change in the water height tells you roughly how strong the current is at a given time, but look at the symbols along the bottom two lines to get more accurate times for maximum slack and flood times.

39

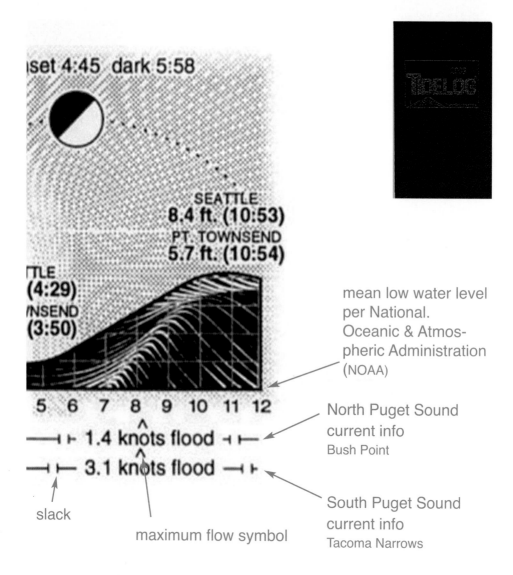

set 4:45 dark 5:58

SEATTLE
8.4 ft. (10:53)
PT. TOWNSEND
5.7 ft. (10:54)

TLE
(4:29)
NSEND
(3:50)

5 6 7 8 9 10 11 12

—|+ 1.4 knots flood ⊣ ⊢—

—|⊢ 3.1 knots flood —|⊢

slack

maximum flow symbol

mean low water level per National. Oceanic & Atmospheric Administration (NOAA)

North Puget Sound current info
Bush Point

South Puget Sound current info
Tacoma Narrows

Figure 11. In Tidelog, the maximum flow and slack are indicated by symbols along the bottom two lines. The upper line is for North Puget sound, and corresponds fairly well to all dive sites described in this book except Titlow Marine Park in the Tacoma Narrows.

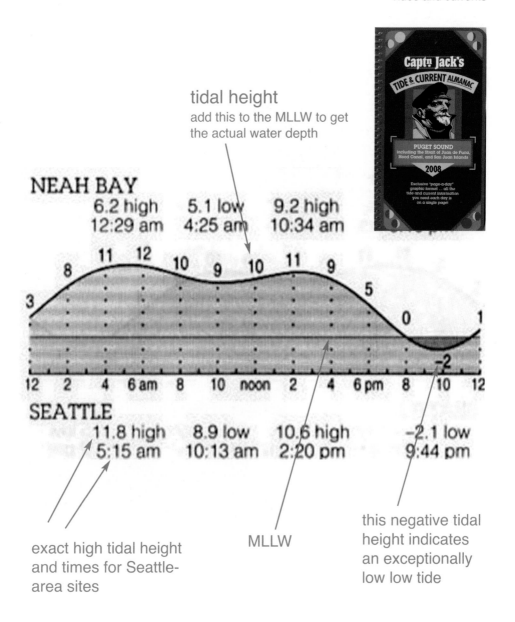

tidal height
add this to the MLLW to get
the actual water depth

NEAH BAY
6.2 high   5.1 low   9.2 high
12:29 am   4:25 am   10:34 am

SEATTLE
11.8 high   8.9 low   10.6 high   −2.1 low
5:15 am   10:13 am   2:20 pm   9:44 pm

exact high tidal height
and times for Seattle-
area sites

MLLW

this negative tidal
height indicates
an exceptionally
low low tide

*Figure 12. Captn Jack's is a popular tidal almanac with easy-
to-use graphics.*

Figure 13. Bull kelp in a 2.2 knot current at Titlow Marine Preserve. It is a constant struggle to stay on course in a current like this.

This diver is swimming against a current above the eelgrass at the Junkyard at Alki.

bent eelgrass.

Site layouts

Edmonds

Seattle

Tacoma

Diving a site for the first time can be daunting. It is frequently unclear where to enter the water, what attractions to look for, and how to keep safe. We usually need to dive a site several times to get a good feel for it. The Alki Pipeline is a great example of how difficult it can be to dive a site properly—even experienced divers have trouble following the pipeline to its end, where the best marine life is found.

Scuba-crazed divers, with lots of free time, will visit a site over and over again until they understand it. But the more causal diver, with a

white buoy at Alki Junkyard

pilings at Titlow Marine Park

bright-colored buoys at Bruce Higgins

jetty tip

water taxi buoys at Seacrest

Figure 1. A variety of surface markers help guide divers at the sites. Make an effort to know their significance.

44

real life outside of diving, can easily get discouraged before being able to appreciate how good a site is. One reason we wrote this book was our own frustration in figuring out how to dive sites properly.

Surface markings
Most of the popular dive sites have one or more fairly obvious surface markers. These could be anything from a solitary buoy, to large wooden pilings (**Figure 1**). In general, the best way to approach a dive is to identify surface markers above water, take a compass reading, and use your compass reading to follow the ocean floor to the area of interest.   Alternatively, you can surface swim to a marker, descend, and then explore the surrounding ocean floor. We much prefer traveling the ocean bottom, as you usually see a lot of good stuff on your way to the site markers.

Following a compass reading underwater, however, is almost always more difficult than one would think. If you think you are near your mark but can't find it, carefully swim to the surface and check. But keep in mind that surfacing when you are lost can be dangerous. It is the principle reason for using a dive flag. Even with a flag, however, making an unplanned surface trip could get you into trouble. Listen for motor boats as you ascend. Keep an upward watch for objects that you might hit.

Once you surface, you should be able to see your surface marker, unless you are *really* far off. This can happen in strong currents, if you have not diligently followed your compass, or if you are simply lost. Whatever the reason, if you can't see your surface marker, you could be seriously disoriented. If you cannot easily figure out where you went wrong, go back to shore—on the surface by sight or along the bottom by compass. Do not remain submerged in deep water for long unless you are sure that you know where you are.

Underwater markers
Many of the sites described here have some sort of underwater markers to help you identify the intended attractions and keep you from getting lost. Rope or steel cables have been set up at most of the sites (**Figure 2**). Make it a priority to find them early in your dive, and use them.   Get as much information about the site layouts and underwater markers before you dive a site: check your most up-to-date

Figure 2. Examples of various ropes used to mark underwater trails. Some, like the one at the Alki Junkyard, are pretty minimal and may not be there by the time you read this book.

dive guides, research the internet, and speak to other divers. In this book, we make only general references to site trails because they are often not rigorously maintained. They can be in a different spot (or gone!) by the time you read this.

Underwater markers need to be maintained. Otherwise, they get hidden by seaweed, upset, or swept away by the currents (**Figures 3 and 4**). Unfortunately, maintenance at most dive sites is not rigorous enough to guarantee that the markers are always functional. Even at Bruce Higgins Underwater Trails, the underwater markers can become non-functional at times. Think. If things don't look like you expected down there, you may be lost. Or things may have changed since whatever you read was written. If things don't look the way you expected, it is a good policy to assume that *you* are having the problem, and may be disoriented. Re-assess the situation. Don't assume anything. This is part of the adventure of shore diving!

Bottom slope

While surface markers and underwater trails are helpful, your most important navigational tool is to pay attention to where you are at all times. Having and using a compass are absolutely essential at most sites. When in doubt about your directions, your vision of the bottom can help. Most of the time, the bottom slopes sharply enough that the direction to shore is obvious (**Figure 5**). However, flat or undulating spots in the ocean floor can fool you. Use your vision *and* your compass to double-check.

hidden trail ropes
Saltwater State Park

Figure 3. These underwater trail ropes are concealed by kelp.

partially hidden trail ropes
Bruce Higgins Underwater Trails

Figure 4. Underwater signs are a nice idea, but they require regular maintenance—something that is not available at most sites. These signs were at Bruce Higgins Underwater Trails.

Figure 5. These divers are 80 feet down at the Alki Junkyard. The steep slope of the ocean floor makes the direction back to shore obvious

Viz

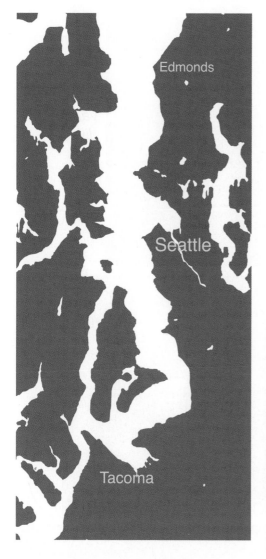

Water visibility, or *viz,* is one of the great mysteries of scuba diving in Puget Sound. It varies hugely from day-to-day and from site-to-site, ranging from 3 to 40+ feet (**Figure 1**). Marine biologists attribute the variation to the *big three*: rain runoff, wind conditions, and plankton bloom (**Figure 2**). The interplay between these complex factors makes day to day viz prediction nearly impossible.

Bad viz days make for less-than ideal underwater sight-seeing. Unfortunately, predicting tomorrow's viz is even tougher than predicting

SO-SO
10 foot viz

Figure 1. Approximate visibility on various dives.

pretty good
20 foot viz

awesome
30 foot viz

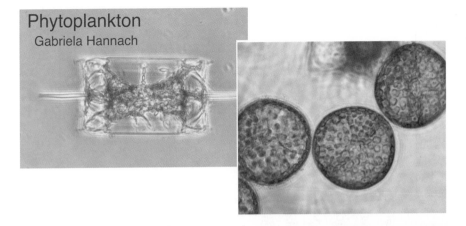

Phytoplankton
Gabriela Hannach

Zooplankton
Kevin Li

Figure 2. There are hundreds of individual phytoplankton and zooplankton in every thimble-full of Puget Sound water. They nourish the incredible variety of larger sea life. They also cut down on the viz.

tomorrow's weather. The effect of last night's rain might be offset by a low plankton bloom, which could be offset by cloudy skies, which could....... You get the idea.

Descending into soup

Water clarity also varies by depth, as a function of temperature changes, and varying plankton concentrations. Viz is generally worse at shallower depths, due to higher plankton counts and particulate matter stirred up by wave action. On a windy day, it is not unusual to have less than 1 foot visibility until you get 5-15 feet under the sur-

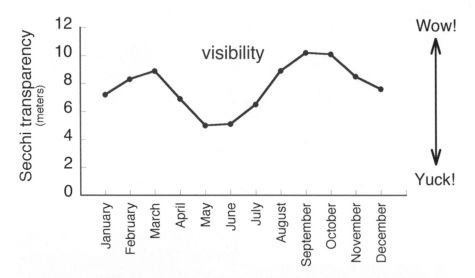

Figure 3. *This graph shows average water clarity from five Puget Sound Marine stations from 2000 through 2007. Remember, these are* **averages**. *You can stumble into good or bad dive conditions on any given day year-round.*

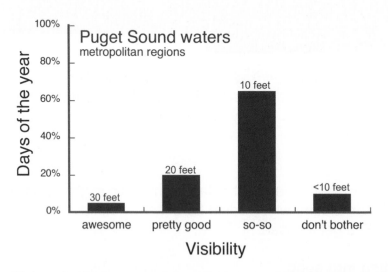

Figure 4. *We're not going to lie to you. Most days, viz is in the 10-15 foot range, meaning that you have to pay attention to what's in front of you so you don't bump into it! Ten feet is decent for observing wildlife, but not very good for appreciating large structures. This graph shows our estimates of viz days per year. It could vary substantially from year to year.*

face. New divers may freak out at the poor viz, without descending low enough to realize that conditions are fine once you descend through the surface layer. Even on a seemingly horrible day at the surface, viz can be pretty good at lower depths. But be careful in unfamiliar sites! When descending in soup, move slowly and be prepared for surprises at close range. Look ahead of you, not to the side for long. These dive conditions can be a little scary at first, but we're usually glad we gave it a chance at lower depths.

Good viz omens
1. limited precipitation
2. low plankton
3. sunny day
4. calm water

The only sure way to know the viz on a given day is to gear up and head down. But you want to know conditions before loading gear and driving to the beach. There are some ways to guesstimate the viz on a given day. Viz tends to be better if it has not rained for a while, the water is calm, and the plankton are down. This constellation of optimal conditions is most likely to occur in the winter and fall. Viz tends to be worst in the spring and early summer, when plankton blooms are greatest (**Figures 3 and 4**). You may do better than guesstimate the viz based on time of year and weather conditions in a couple of ways. First, call your local dive shop or scuba-crazed friends and ask about the day's conditions. Second, you can check internet-connected monitoring sites.

The City of Seattle and King County, in conjunction with the Seattle Aquarium and other agencies, are developing an increasingly sophisticated system of water-monitoring sites to track water temperature, pH, oxygenation, chlorophyll, and turbidity. The details of how the data is presented will likely change by the time you read this book, but the websites help you to figure out how to use the information to get a rough idea of what the viz will be on a given day. The informational format will be a little too technical for some users, but it will hopefully be simplified in the near future. As of October, 2008, you can reach the website at http:// dnr.metrokc.gov/wlr/ waterres/marine/HiFrequency.htm. It is also findable, with some effort, through the King County website: www.kingcounty.gov.

real-time underwater WEBcam images,

salmon spawning stream

Figure 5. Joe Weiss teaches environmental and marine science at the Marine Technology Center st Seahurst Park in Burien. The site includes a salmon hatchery and ocean monitoring station. Thanks to the Highline School District for supporting this center.

saltwater salmon tanks

fresh water salmon tanks

The use of technology to monitor oceanic conditions is growing rapidly. Another example of a scuba-friendly water quality informational resource is the Marine Science Seahurst Observatory in Burien. It also includes a web-based monitoring site to show dive conditions real-time. Built by oceanographers and engineers from the University of Washington's Applied Physics Laboratory and the Puget Sound Skill Center's Environmental and Marine Science Program, the underwater station itself includes monitoring gear and some reef structure (**Figure 5**). The station provides real-time water condition data and video. To improve the station's utility, Joe Weiss has collaborated with colleagues from the University of Washington to add underwater visibility gauges (Secchi disks) that help users assess water conditions (**Figure 9**). To appreciate its potential and the limitations of the website for assessing the day's dive conditions, it is best to monitor the site for a few days (or scan archived images).

Who ya gonna call?

Like any underwater structure, the Seahurst Observatory is subject to degradation by nature and humans. If you want to dive The Node, it is a good idea to check with Joe Weiss first.

phone: 206 433 2107
email: psscmarinelab@gmail.com

The details of how the camera is marked and what information is displayed on the website may change by the time you read this. As of September, 2008, the site's web address is www.seahurst.apl. washington.edu/index.php. Or you can reach it via links from the Burien Parks and Recreation website: www.burienwa.gov.

If you plan to dive the station to see it for yourself, it is a good idea to check with Joe first. Partly to find out if there are substantial changes from what you read here, and partly to find out if there is something you can do to help while you're down there (**Figure 10**).

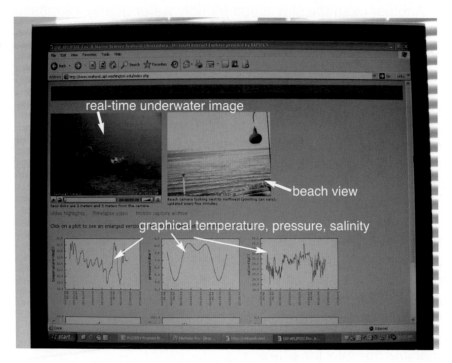

Figure 6. The Observatory website displays real-time under-water images, along with water condition data.

if you go...

The ocean floor at Seahurst Park is not included as one of the eleven dive sites in this book. Apart from a nearly-gone sunken barge, there is little here for divers to explore. However, some readers may choose to check out the underwater node.

If you decide to check the observatory out for yourself, be ready for some serious exercise. There is no public automobile access to the Marine Technology Center. You have to park at the lower Seahurst lot and carry your gear to the beach at the Center (**Figure 7**). For us, this means three trips with a dolly. Or you can walk the distance fully geared up...but check with your cardiologist first.

Marine Technology Center

lower Seahurst Parking lot

←— long walk —→

Figure 7. Aerial view of Seahurst park. (Photo from the Washington State Department of Ecology)

small buoy may mark camera site (9/08)

The underwater video cam site may be marked by a small buoy. If you plan to visit the underwater site, it is a good idea to check first with Joe Weiss regarding site markings.

section of fishing net

15 foot MLLW

Figure 8. The underwater node site includes some artificial reef structure and a variety of electronic gear.

junction box

buried cable leads back to shore

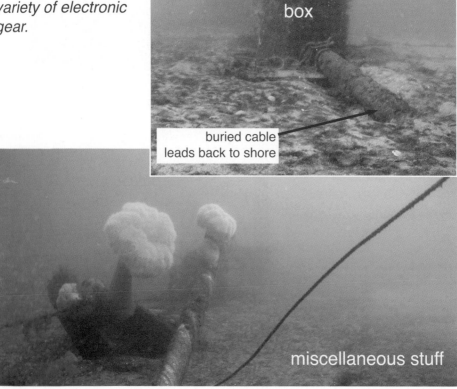

miscellaneous stuff

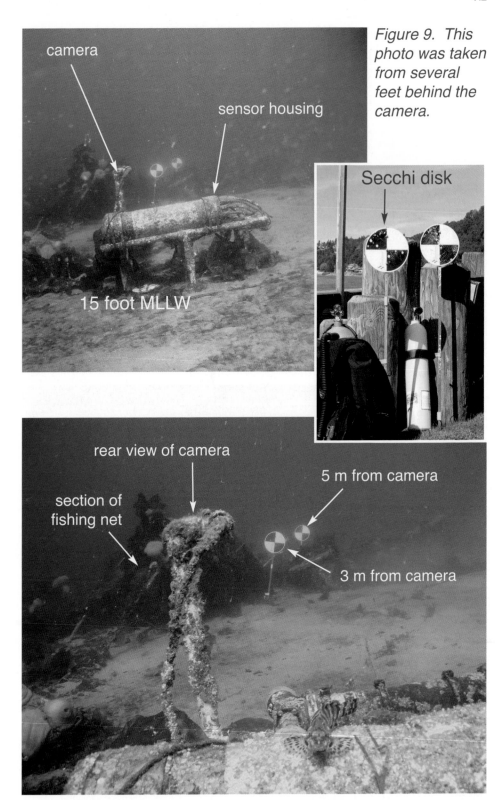

camera

sensor housing

Figure 9. This photo was taken from several feet behind the camera.

Secchi disk

15 foot MLLW

rear view of camera

5 m from camera

section of fishing net

3 m from camera

Figure 10. One problem with maintaining underwater cameras is the constant growth of algae and seaweed on the equipment. If you go down to check this out, please gently wipe the lens if there is obvious plant growth. You might also check with Joe ahead of time to see if something else needs attending to down there.

Changes

Internet-based options to assess the day's dive conditions will likely expand considerably in the next few years. Web addresses listed here are merely examples to show you what may be available.

Photography

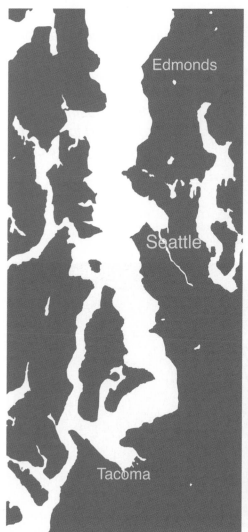

U nderwater photography is one of the joys of diving. We love collecting pictures of marine life and structures down there. Like above-water photography, the introduction of digital cameras has made marine photography relatively easy, even for very casual photographers. This chapter is here partly to encourage you to try underwater photography, and partly to explain some of the not-so-great-quality shots you'll see throughout this book. The nitty-gritties of marine photography can get pretty involved, and are way beyond the scope of this book. But for amateurs like us, who can take some decent photos, there are a few points worth making.

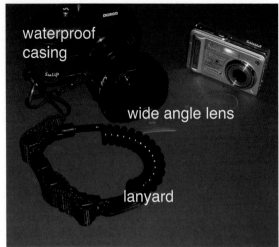

Figure 1. Underwater camera systems typically include a specially-formatted digital camera, with a water-tight housing. The lanyard is used to attach the camera to your BCD. Use one.

waterproof casing

wide angle lens

lanyard

Figure 2. Rear view.

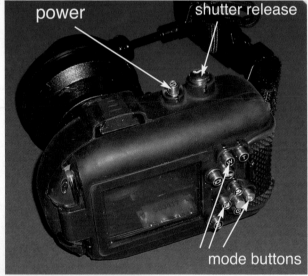

power

shutter release

mode buttons

Figure 3. Rear view of water-tight case. The mode buttons, which can be operated underwater, overlay the mode buttons on the back of any modern digital camera.

Apart from learning how to work through a waterproof housing, operating a digital camera underwater is almost as easy as it is topside. The photos in this book were taken with standard, relatively inexpensive cameras.

Most underwater camera systems are comprised of a main body and an outer waterproof housing (**Figures 1-3**). The main bodies are either standard off-the-shelf models, or models that have added software features to correct for color loss underwater.

The biggest underwater photographic problem is the corrosive effect of seawater. The deeper you take a camera, the more likely that any imperfection in its seals will allow a few drops of water in. Unfortunately, electronic gear is exquisitely sensitive to the corrosive effects of saltwater. The damage is immediate and *permanent*. We have learned this the hard, *expensive* way. The seals need to be inspected before *each* use. Make sure to read (and follow) instructions regarding maintenance of your waterproof housing.

Types of underwater cameras
There are many underwater camera models available though your local dive shop, some general photographic retailers, and many internet companies (**Figures 4-7**). Low-end, reliable cameras start at about $150. Higher-end systems go for $1,000 on up. Newer systems that incorporate an outer housing *and* a water-proof regular housing are probably worth their cost in preventing a wipeout of the camera if the outer housing leaks. Underwater digital photography is a fast-moving industry. Chances are that the models shown in Figures 4-7 will have long ago been replaced by the time you read this.

Photo finishing
Second only to its efficiency, the next biggest advantage of digital over film photography is film-finishing software. Most photos in this book have been color-adjusted using readily available software. The programs adjust the image for loss of reds, yellows and blues as sunlight traverses the water (**Figures 8-10**). More advanced features allow image sharpening, contrast, etc. Most photos in this book have been color-adjusted only. With a little effort, you could improve substantially on what you'll see here.

Figure 4.
Intova
rated to 180' depth
6.0 mega-pixel
AA batteries

Figure 5.
Sea&Sea
rated to 150' depth
6.2 mega-pixel
rechargeable Li battery

Figure 6.
Sea&Sea
rated to 164' depth
10 mega-pixel
rechargeable Li battery

Figure 7.
Olympus
doubly waterproof camera—the
main body is waterproof to 33 feet,
providing a layer of protection in
case the outer case leaks.

Figure 8. This photo of the Alki Pipeline opening was taken at a depth of 40 feet. The image on the left is untouched, and dominated by greens. The image on the right was touched-up with Photoshop, accentuating the reds, blues and yellows. This photo was taken on a sunny day. No flash was used, because the subject is too far away for the flash to reach.

Deep water photography

There are two problems with taking photos in deeper water. The first is simple loss of light, such that the images are dark. Longer exposure times that would produce lighter images are not generally practical, because keeping a camera still underwater is difficult. The second problem with deeper photography is the progressive loss of reds, oranges, yellows, greens and blues as sunlight traverses the water. This loss of color gives the image an overwhelming green hue as you descend. For photos taken down to 40 feet depths, the color loss can be partially digitally corrected with photographic software. But at greater depths, where digital correction is not possible, only greens or grays remain. Deeper than 40 feet you must have a flash to get reasonable color (**Figures 11 and 12**) .

Standard-issue built-in digital camera flashes are not much good underwater, as they scatter light back into the lens. Avoiding flash

Figure 9. This photo shows an earthmover tire (the "Enhance-ments") at Bruce Higgins Underwater Trails. The image on the left is untouched, and dominated by greens. The image on the right was color-adjusted with Photoshop, accentuating the reds, yellows and blues. The contrast was increased slightly.

Figure 10. This photo shows the original and the color-ad-justed photo of a tube worm bouquet on Slinky at Bruce Hig-gins Underwater Trails. The image on the left is untouched, and dominated by greens.

8 feet from subject
no flash
40 foot depth

2 feet from subject
with flash
40 foot depth

Figure 11. The top photo of a diver behind a reef ball at the Alki Junkyard was taken without a flash. Other than the diver's flashlight, only greens show up. To the right is a photo taken at close range with a flash, so that the colors show up fully.

backscatter requires a system to hold the flash away from the camera—the further the better (**Figure 13**). With flash photography you can get spectacular color shots in deeper water. Upgrading from point-and-shoot to underwater flash photography, however, entails a substantial increase in sophistication and cost.

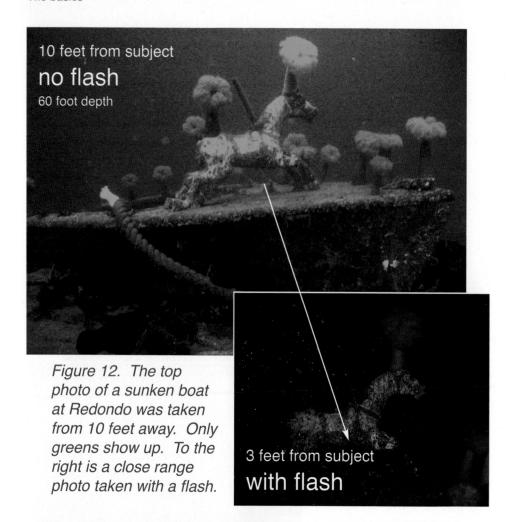

10 feet from subject
no flash
60 foot depth

3 feet from subject
with flash

Figure 12. The top photo of a sunken boat at Redondo was taken from 10 feet away. Only greens show up. To the right is a close range photo taken with a flash.

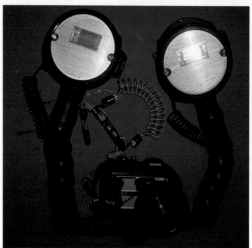

Figure 13. Sealife 600 with double flashes. This model was used for most of the flash photography seen throughout this book.

Even the best flashes will only travel about 8 feet in Puget Sound water. Some of the deeper structure shots in this book are deeply green, since they had to be taken from a distance to capture the entire structure of interest.

Safety

Edmonds

Seattle

Tacoma

We love scuba diving. It's interesting, it's fun, and it's challenging. It's also what insurers consider an *inherently dangerous sport*. It has been said that you are more likely to hurt yourself bowling than scuba diving. That may be true. The important difference, though, is that typical bowling injuries include sprains or bruises; diving accidents have more dire consequences. When things go wrong, they can *really* go wrong. Much of the dive literature plays down the inherent danger of scuba. Not a good idea. Along with all of the great things about diving here we think it is wise

view from beach

view at water level

Figure 1. These two views of the ferry pilings at Titlow are a good example of why panic can set in if you get into trouble away from shore—surface structures look much further away at water level than they do from a higher perspective. You have to take all safety tips seriously. If you run into trouble and have to surface, the way back will seem a lot further than it looked from the beach.

to acknowledge openly that some very bad things can, and do, happen to divers.

All divers should be familiar with basic scuba safety learned during open water certification. There are many basic scuba courses and books available. We are not going to to use space here to duplicate what is widely available elsewhere. The following are a few additional safety issues specific to safe Puget Sound shore-diving.

This is serious diving

Perhaps the first safety lesson is to acknowledge that shore diving is serious diving. Even though the reef structure at most of the dive spots described here is just offshore, once you leave shore and look around at water level, things appear very far away (**Figure 1**). Getting into trouble out there will put you into a situation that will appear much more frightening than you might think. Take your safety training seriously.

Do your homework
Learn about the attractions and the dangers of the site beforehand. Talk with others who have dived the site. Start with experts at your dive shop. Talk with divers you meet at the site—many of them love to yack away. Talk to more than one diver and check that their advice is consistent; we've occasionally received misleading advice from divers who either didn't know what they were talking about, or were pulling our legs.

Read this book and other local dive books. Each author gives a different perspective on each site. You can also get a feel for some dive sites by searching the Net. But be aware that internet reviews may be outdated or reflect the prejudice of some unusual individuals.

Limit your depth
There is no doubt that the deeper you dive, the less likely it is that you could make it safely to the surface if something went wrong. How deep is *safe* and how deep do you need to go? Open water certification is intended for depths to 60 feet, and most of the interesting marine life you'll see in Puget sound is within 60 feet of the surface. The only site described in this book that would take you deeper are the I-beams at Alki Cove 2. They start at about 85 feet MLLW, and we do not advise you to check them out unless you have advanced training. Regardless of your certification, if you find yourself more than 60 feet down, you are deeper and further from shore than the sites described in this book call for.

Currents
Tidal flows can be quite strong and potentially dangerous, depending on the site and when you dive it. Currents in Puget Sound generally run parallel to shore, but there can be significant directional deviations due to the shape of the nearby shore (see Chapter 5). You can get a rough idea of the potential for dangerous currents simply by looking at a map to see how narrow the Sound is at the site you plan to dive. Typical maximum flows of 1.5 knots occur at sites like Les Davis, Alki

bent eelgrass.

Figure 2. This smart diver is starting his dive against the current, evidenced by the bending eelgrass.

and Three Tree. In contrast, water speeds can exceed 4 knots at Titlow Marine Park at the Tacoma Narrows.

Diving at any site is more fun if you plan your dive around slack times (see Chapter 5). *No one* can swim comfortably for long against a current greater than one knot. If you are diving in a substantial current, always swim against it on the first half of the dive, and with it upon your return. We *never* knowingly swim *with* the current in the first half of our dive.

To check current flow at the start of your dive, observe movement of plant life—eelgrass, bull kelp, or seaweed are good indicators (**Figure 2**). If they are anything other than straight up, there is a current. If there is no flexible plant life to observe, do not assume that there is no current. Look for *something* to indicate the flow. It is very easy to swim *with* a current without realizing it, until you try to go back!

Currents tend to be weaker near the bottom. If you're not careful and do get stuck swimming against a current when you're tired, stay near the bottom on your way back to shore. If you can't make it back to your entry point, head for a nearer shore point or buoy and signal for help. Don't wait until you are tired, low on air, or far from shore.

Know where you're at
It is amazing how quickly you can get directionally challenged (lost) underwater. Keep constantly aware of the direction back to shore, and always have a rough idea of how far away you are.

At most sites in this book, the bottom slope makes the direction to shore obvious. However, there are regions at all these dive sites where the bottom slopes so gently that you can't use it to figure out your direction back to shore. And at some sites, like the Pipeline at Alki and Bruce Higgins Underwater Trails, the ocean floor is so flat that a compass reading is the only way to be sure of your direction. When in doubt, surface carefully to make sure you know the direction back to shore.

Equipment problems
Apart from the numerous unlikely equipment failures that you learn about in open water certification, there are a couple of BCD problems that we've experienced or heard about. One particularly dangerous situation is to charge your air system, turn it off, and then forget to turn it back on before entering the water. Doing so leaves you with a breath or two of air—just enough to descend a few feet before real-izing that you cannot inflate your BCD to stop your descent. While dropping a few weights could bring you back up, a moment of panic could be fatal.

Empty tank
Really dumb, but it happens. Running low on air can get you into all kinds of trouble—too far from shore in a strong current, unable to make a safety stop on the way up, etc. Remember, you are diving in deep, cold water, a situation where you will use air faster. Throw in the distraction of some unusual marine life, and you can find yourself low on air and far from shore. Remember that you need enough air to get back to the surface *and* enough to make it back to shore.

The 1/3 tank rule is a good one: 1/3 to get where you are going, 1/3 to return, and 1/3 left in case of emergency. Sure, it's tempting to push the limit to maximize your dive time. But, better safe than sorry. Bring a second tank and plan for two dives rather than maxing out a single tank.

Working with gloves on
The cold Puget Sound water makes thick neoprene gloves an absolute essential. They do a pretty good job keeping your hands warm enough throughout a dive. However, if anything goes wrong with your equipment, fixing it while wearing gloves can turn an easy task into a nearly-impossible one.

Thick gloves make it difficult to distinguish parts of your gear, especially if they are not in your field of vision. Think about simple tasks that would be easy above water: adjusting straps, locating a knife, dropping weights, or finding the regulator that just slipped out of your mouth. Performing simple tasks like these 60 feet down with limited peripheral vision and wearing thick gloves can be much, much harder than you expect. Run through some equipment failure scenarios at shallow depths. Toss your regulator back and try to find it. Make sure you can reach your weight release. Try pulling that knife out of its sheath without dropping it.

The Alki pipeline

West Seattle

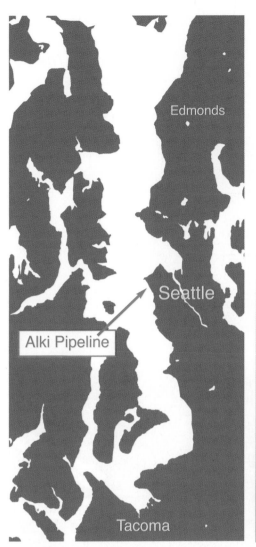

The Pipeline at Alki is a storm drain that doubles as a sewer overflow during heavy rains. The sewer function is left over from earlier times when raw sewage was routinely emptied directly into the sound. Fortunately, that only occurs a few times a year now. The area is officially known as Charles Richey Sr. Viewpoint at Alki Beach Park. It is a city-designated marine preserve, prohibiting any collection of marine life.

The Pipeline, as it is locally referred to, has it all. It is a relatively shallow dive with enough sunlight to photograph lots of brightly colored

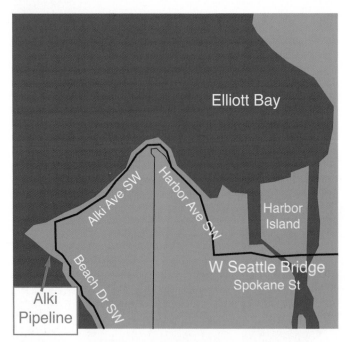

Figure 1. The Pipeline is on Beach Dr. SW, just around the bend of Alki Point.

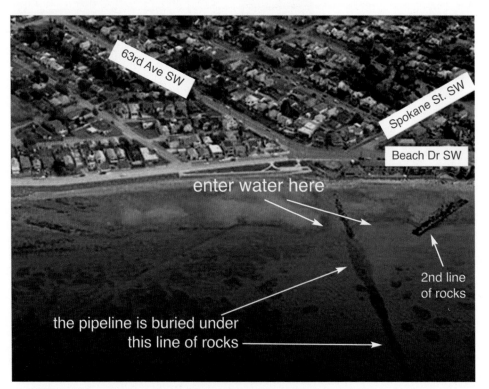

Figure 2. Aerial view of the Pipeline at Alki. (Photo from the Washington State Department of Ecology)

marine life, concentrated here because the pipeline and its covering of large rocks provide lots of reef structure. The pipe's mouth, about 100 yards from shore, is a large structure that hosts many critters and the occasional large lingcod. On a sunny, good viz day, this dive could be mistaken for something from the tropics. And the site is shallow enough that your tank should last a long time.

The biggest drawback to the site is the long swim to the opening, but there's plenty here to see even without going to the end of the pipeline. Another drawback with this site is that it is surprisingly difficult to follow the pipe to its end. The pipeline is covered for its first half by a mound of large rocks (**Figure 2**). The section near shore is a *can't miss*. But further out, the line dips below the sand and there are no rocks over it. Even experienced divers can lose the line of the pipe once it disappears, and not be able to locate the next section when it emerges from the sand about 30 yards further out (**Figure 11**). We dove this site four times before getting comfortable with locating the end.

Getting there
The Pipeline is at the northwest corner of West Seattle. Exit I-5 at the the West Seattle Bridge. Take the Harbor Ave exit and follow along the water until it turns into Alki Ave SW. Alki Ave SW turns into Beach Dr SW after rounding Alki Point. The pipeline pumphouse is located where 63rd Ave SW and Spokane St meet at Beach Dr (**Figures 1 and 2**).

Parking
Parking is usually convenient. The party crowd stays north along Alki Beach. With a little luck, you can park at the curb, right in front of the site (**Figure 3**). Gear up at your car and walk to the beach. Or carry you gear to the concrete wall and gear up there (**Figure 6**).

Amenities
Not much. Maybe a portable pottie. The closest shower is 0.8 miles east on Alki Ave SW (**Figure 4**). There are many restaurants near the Junkyard and Seacrest Park, about a mile east on Alki Ave SW (see Chapters 13 and 19).

looking north along Beach Dr SW

Figure 3. View of the park, looking southwest. There's usually ample parking available on Beach Dr. SW, immediately in front of the Park.

Figure 4. These public bathrooms and shower are located 0.8 miles east on Beach Dr SW/Alki Ave SW.

shower

Reef structure

The pipeline and the rocks that cover it. The massiveness of the structure and the vast amount of marine life that calls it home are truly remarkable.

Surface landmarks

The most important landmark at the Pipeline is the line of rocks starting at the beach. Take a careful compass reading and use it to help you stay on course (**Figure 11**). The buoy at the end of the pipeline is a good landmark, but it is a long way out.

Swimming to the reef

Enter the water on either side of the rocks covering the pipeline (**Figures 2 and 7-10**). It is important that you stay over or close to the line of rocks. If you lose the rock line, it is difficult to re-orient yourself without going back towards shore.

You could surface swim to the white buoy and follow the chain down, but this is a long swim that looks intimidating at water level from the shore. In choppy water, the buoy may not be easily visible when you are at the surface! And you would miss all the marine life along the way.

Currents

The currents are relatively moderate here. Alki Point juts out into the sound just north of this dive site, forming a headland. It interferes with current flow, setting up lesser eddy currents north and south of the point.

Hazards

This is a good site at which to use a dive flag, because you'll be a long way from shore, where boaters won't expect divers (note the large sailboat not far beyond the buoy in **Figure 9)**. We strongly advise you to not venture past the end of the pipeline, because you would be getting very, very far from shore.

This site has a wide open southern exposure and the surf can be rough in windy weather. We have dived this site in bad surf, and the view back to shore in rough conditions can look downright frightening!

park mural
Lezlie Jane and Iris Nichols

The Intertidal World

Constellation Park
Marine Reserve

WARNING
Toxic
Shellfish
Shellfish from this area
are unsafe to eat due
paralytic shellfish tox
Do not eat clams,oyste
mussels or scallops.

Red Tide Hotline
1-800-562-5632

sidewalk sculpture
Lezlie Jane

WARNING
Eating shellfish or crabs from this area may
make you sick. And, Seattle Parks Code says:
do not take shellfish,crab & seaweed from here.

WARNING
Possible Sewage Overflows
During and Following Heavy Rain

Questions? Call: 206-205-1151
Regarding CSO #K053

Figure 5. The park has a tiled wall mural and a sidewalk sculpture depicting some of the sea life you'll see.

Figure 6. This concrete wall is a great place to gear up, before walking down to the water.

You know you're in trouble when...

If you are trying to visit the end of the pipeline, you should be within sight of the overlying rocks along the way, except for the short stretch toward the end of the pipeline.

Marine life

The area is a marine preserve, with a phenomenal variety of marine life. The shallowness makes this a great site for photography, especially on sunny days.

looking north

Figure 7. This is the view looking north from the dive site. Most of the beach is covered at high tide.

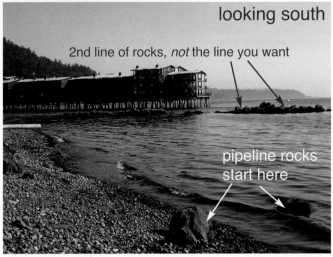

looking south

2nd line of rocks, *not* the line you want

pipeline rocks start here

Figure 8. This is the view looking south from the dive site. The second line of rocks in the distance is **not** the one you want!

buoy

Figure 9. This is the view straight out from the beach. Notice the sailboat passing just beyond the buoy. Use a flag here.

Figure 10. This view from the pumphouse shows rocks covering the shallow part of the pipeline. These proximal rocks are not visible at high tide. The buoy looks pretty far away— it is!

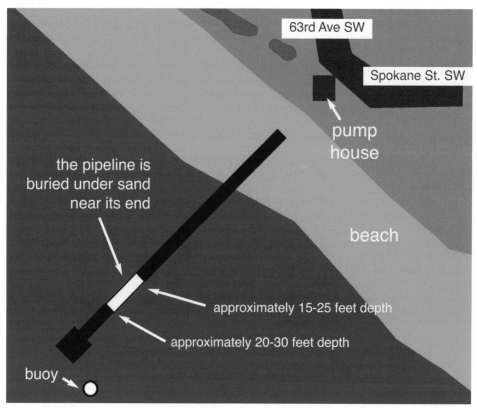

63rd Ave SW

Spokane St. SW

pump
house

the pipeline is
buried under sand
near its end

beach

approximately 15-25 feet depth

approximately 20-30 feet depth

buoy

Figure 11. Schematic of major structures, relative to the beach. It is easy to lose your way when the pipeline disappears under the sand. Once you get off course, it's difficult to get back on. Faced with that situation, we cautiously go to the surface and head for the buoy (if we can see it).

buoy chain

buoy

seaweed
on chain

this concrete block anchors the buoy
near the end of the pipeline
approximately 25-35 feet depth

this is the view
up the buoy line

rocky bottom near shore
8-18 feet depth

concrete junction box
0-10 feet depth

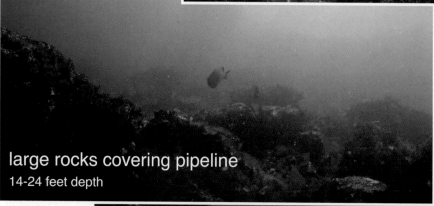

large rocks covering pipeline
14-24 feet depth

sandy bottom next to pipeline
14-24 feet depth

lawn ornament

18-28 feet depth

lawn ornament

18-28 feet depth

Figure 12. A couple of lawn orna-
ments have been placed in the
sand overlying the buried portion
of the pipeline. (We can't guarantee they will be there by the time
you read this book)

sand and eelgrass, to side of pipeline

12-22 feet depth

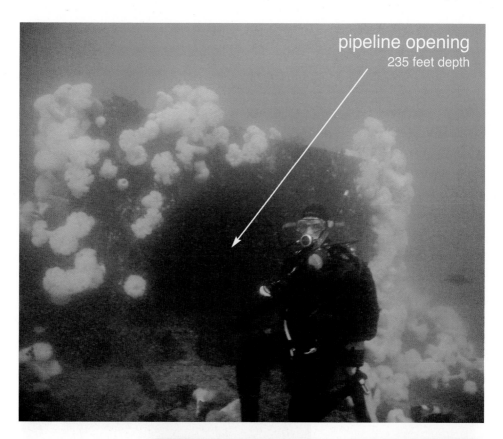

pipeline opening
235 feet depth

Figure 13. It is well worth the effort to swim out to the end of the Pipeline.

distant view of opening

kelp crab
20-30 feet depth

plumose anemone bouquet
20-30 feet depth

orange sea pen
50-60 feet depth
(this was past the end of the pipeline)

quillback rockfish
12-22 feet depth

sea lettuce field
15-25 feet depth

sea lettuce

rockweed

brittle stars
10-20 feet depth

diver's
glove

Turkish towel

giant anemone
20-30 feet depth

giant anemone
15-25 feet depth

brittle star
10-20 feet depth

giant plumose anemones
22-32 feet depth

diver's
glove

nudibranch
white-lined dirona
20-30 feet depth

diver's
finger

nudibranch
variable dendronotid
15-25 feet depth

diver's palm

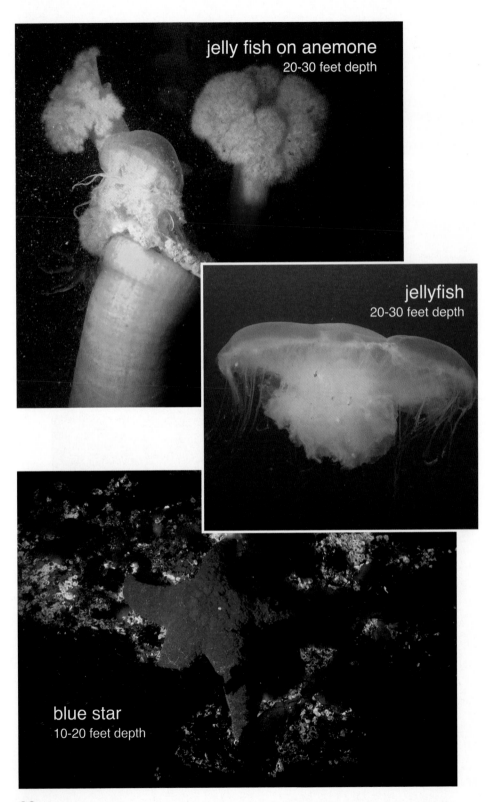

jelly fish on anemone
20-30 feet depth

jellyfish
20-30 feet depth

blue star
10-20 feet depth

Some ways that the Pipeline at Alki dive site may change by the time you read this

We are unaware of any changes to be made at this dive site in the foreseeable future. That's fine by us.

Bruce Higgins
Underwater
Trails

Edmonds

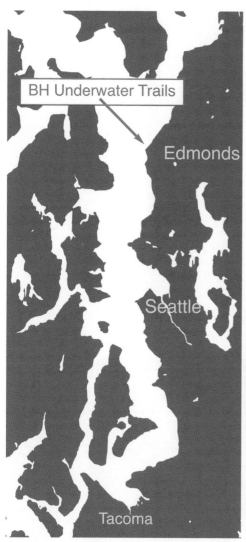

Bruce Higgins Underwater Trails, formerly known as the Edmonds Underwater Park, was established by the City of Edmonds in 1970. It includes approximately 30 acres of tidal and subtidal land, designated as a Marine Protected Area. Any taking of marine life from the park is prohibited. No boats.

Before we get started with the scuba details, we want to make it clear to you that this is an *amazing* place. It has more life and more interesting structure than any other dive spot in Puget Sound. The fishing and boating bans have been shockingly successful at marine preser-

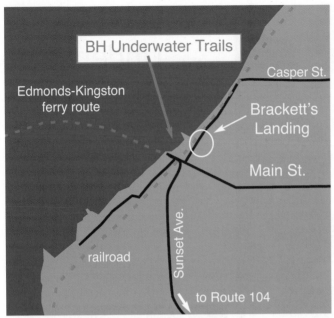

Figure 1. Brackett's Landing is adjacent to the Edmonds-Kingston ferry terminal, on the Edmonds waterfront.

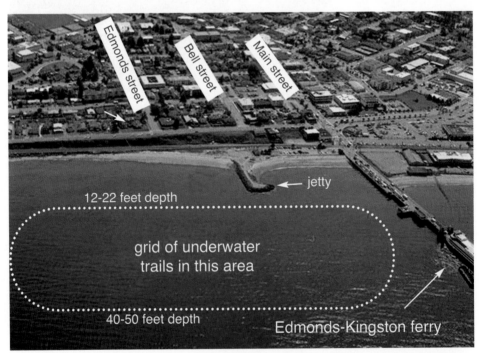

Figure 2. Aerial view of the Bruce Higgins Underwater Trails site. The region of underwater trails is approximated by the dotted lines. (Photo from the Washington State Department of Ecology)

102

lingcod
15-25 feet depth

Figure 3. We're not kidding about the ling-cod! They typically lounge around, oblivious to nearby divers. This guy did not move until one of us grabbed the steering wheel.

EDMONDS
UNDERWATER PARK
MARINE CONSERVATION AREA

CLOSED TO ALL HARVEST
SEE CURRENT W.D.F.W. PAMPHLET
Enforced By City Of Edmonds Ordinance#2531
DIVERS ALERT NETWORK EMERGENCIES
1-919-684-8111

vation, allowing a surprisingly large number of surprisingly large fish to flourish. The most common are lingcod, which lounge around the place with little concern for divers, until they get within a foot or two. This is the only shore dive site where you will routinely see large numbers of large lingcod. Diving this site offers a glimmer of hope that we can still save the Sound.

In addition to its striking fish population, this is a diver's paradise. The park is a grid of underwater trails that connect a variety of whimsical artificial reef structures. The structures attract marine life and are downright fun to explore.

Great reef structure and abundant marine life. Convenient parking, easy beach access, change rooms and a shower. Life is good. This

How the Park got started

In 1935, the Black Ball Line ferry operators sank the DeLeon Dry Dock about 50 feet north of the current ferry landing area, to impede movement of sand into the dredged-out area. The drydock attracted sea life, which in turn attracted scuba divers. Unfortunately, some of those divers brought spear guns.

Jim McMahan and Bob Barringer, then owners of the Lake City Dive School, first proposed the Underwater Park at a 1970 Edmonds city council meeting. Their main motivation was to protect marine life from being completely depleted by aggressive diver-hunters. To bolster their case, they took councilman Gary Nelson, city attorney Jim Murphy and mayor Harve Harrison for a dive. Impressed with what they saw, they fostered an ordinace passage to establish the site as the first municipal dive park in the USA. Initially, the sunken dry dock was the entire Underwater Park. Today, divers are encouraged to stay north of the DeLeon, due to safety concerns.

Harve Harrison
4-term Edmonds mayor
Mayor Harrison began his diving career with his guided tour of the sunken drydock. He continued to dive into his mid-70s.

Gary Nelson
city councilman

Gary Nelson, past Edmonds City councilman and state legislator, was afflicted with polio at age 29, leaving him with severe leg and left arm weakness. Determined to overcome his handicap, he took up scuba diving as a way to rehabilitate his limbs.

Jim Murphy
city attorney

Jim negotiated a maze of regulatory agencies to make the park a reality. Diving regularly from his 30s into his 70s, he is the first of three generations of Murphy divers.

Park Pitfalls

1. This place is big—you can use up a lot of air just getting to the trail system.

2. It's pretty easy to get lost here. The bottom slopes gently, so the direction to shore is often not obvious.

3. Overgrown seaweed can obscure the trails.

4. The ferry dock is hazardous for divers—know where it is and stay away.

park is a great example of what city leaders and committed volunteers can do to enhance life for the rest of us.

So now you know. We love this park and have dived it many times. However, as great as this place is, it's also important to understand that this is a *serious* dive spot. There are a few pitfalls of which you need to be aware (see Pitfall Box).

The park has been maintained by the volunteer efforts of many individuals, the most dedicated of whom has been Bruce Higgins. His is an inspiring story of a single-minded individual who has donated his own time and organizational skills to build the most interesting underwater park in North America.

Getting there
Bruce Higgins Underwater Trails is at the Edmonds waterfront. Take the State Route 104 exit from I-5 and follow it down to the Edmonds Ferry Terminal. Pay attention as you drive down SR104, because it does a number of twists and turns, with name changes to Edmonds Way and then to Sunset Avenue. Just north of the ferry terminal is the entrance to Brackett's Landing Beach (**Figures 2, 5 and 6**).

Parking
Convenient, but tight at busy times. There are about 35 spots right at the waterfront. If you go at peak user times, you may have to wait

Figure 4. **Bruce Higgins** has lead volunteer efforts at Bruce Higgins Underwater Trails for over 30 years. He learned to dive at the University of Michigan in 1970, and worked in the research dive program until 1973. Bruce worked with Oregon State University's Ocean Engineering Dive Program from 1973 to 1976 and then with Shoreline Community College's Scuba Program, managing it from 1984 to 1991. He worked in NAUI Instructor Training programs from 1984 through 1994.

Today, Bruce describes himself as a recreational diver. He is a computer support expert by profession.

Bruce's dedicated parking spot

volunteers on site, prepping to sink the *Blue Water*

for a spot, or park several blocks away. If the spots are all taken, there is a drop-off area where you can unload your gear quickly and move your car to a side street.

Amenities

Awesome. Bathrooms, change rooms and a shower. Many nearby restaurants. If you go eat at one after your dive, please move your car to a side street.

Reef structure

The park is most famous for its extensive eclectic collection of underwater reef structures situated along the system of underwater trails. The trails are marked with different styles of rope, to help check your position against the map (**Figure 13**). The underwater structures are attractive to humans and to sea creatures. We can't get enough time here to explore it all.

At the south of the park is an old drydock, almost adjacent to the ferry dock. These two long structures attract wildlife, and are interesting to explore. But be careful to stay clear of the ferry dock. In the early days of the park, the drydock was the primary structure of interest. There are now so many other attractions that few divers visit the drydock, due to its proximity to the ferry traffic.

It is a must that you study the system of trails before exploring the park. Get a laminated map at the nearby Underwater Sports dive shop on Railroad Ave. The trail system may seem simple topside, but you can become confused rapidly once you are submerged! Don't lose your map—use a lanyard to fasten it to your wrist or BCD. The maps are available for $15, and the money goes back into park maintenance. Buy a couple of extras to give as Seattle souvenirs.

Surface landmarks

The best landmark is the jetty. A system of buoys is moored at trail junctions. While it is possible to surface swim from one buoy to another, most would consider such surface swims fairly tiring. It is far more practical to use the underwater trails to navigate, rather than the surface buoys.

Figure 5. This is the entrance to Brackett's Landing, coming off of Route 104 (Sunset Ave at this point), just before boarding the Kingston Ferry. Finding an open parking spot can be problematic on warm weather weekends.

Figure 6. This is the sidewalk between the parking lot and the beach. Most divers gear up at their cars and walk to the beach. But there are convenient benches and stone walls to gear up along the sidewalk.

Park Regulations

1. All scuba divers and free divers must dive with a buddy
2. All divers must be certified or in training
3. All divers must wear buoyancy compensation
4. No fish or marine organisms may be harmed or removed from the park
5. No possession of devices used for the taking of fish or other marine life, excepting dive knives
6. No night diving (after 10 PM) without a permit (permits are issued at the Parks and Recreation Office (425 771 0231) between 8 AM and 5 PM M-F.
7. No boats, watercraft or submersible vehicles of any kind are allowed inside the park.

Swimming to the reef

The best way to enter the water is to walk straight down the beach from the parking lot, to the south of the jetty. We usually swim to the end of the jetty and pick up Jetty Way Trail (see **Figures 12 and 14**). From there, follow whatever route you like. Considering the size of the park, we think it is a good idea to plan your route ahead of time.

Currents

The sound widens at Edmonds, so currents are moderate here. However, you still have to be careful during times of high tidal exchange because even moderate currents can make the long swim out to the trails and back tiring. We usually submerge as we walk out from the beach, and stay down for our whole dive. Alternatively, you can surface swim to one of the buoys that marks a trail intersection, but the surface swim can be tiring, especially against a current.

Hazards

Boats are prohibited within the park, so few divers bother with a dive flag. This assumes that you won't wander outside of the park.

The ferry lane is an issue. It is both dangerous and illegal to dive at the ferry lane. A sunken dry dock (DeLeon) just north of the ferry was the original highlight of this site. It is a massive structure that attracts a lot of marine life, but is less visited now since there is so much other structure. Swimming south of the DeLeon will put you right next to the ferry. That would place you at risk of personal injury and in trouble with the police, Coast Guard, and Homeland Security. This is serious!

Be mindful to keep enough air to swim back along the bottom, minimizing your exposure to currents. Take our word for it, a surface swim from the outer edge of the park after running out of air can be a panic-inspiring experience. The outer (west) edge of the park perimeter is much further from shore than any other dive described in this book!

Probably the most daunting aspect of the park is the relatively flat sea floor. The flatness allows the Park to be as big as it is without going too deep. But it also means that you don't have the obvious drop-off to indicate what direction you are headed. Without a map and careful attention to your compass, you can get lost quickly. This is a serous issue! We have gotten lost and wound up further from shore than we

Figure 7. This is a view of the jetty, taken from the parking lot sidewalk. Most divers enter the water from the beach here. But you can also walk north of the jetty and enter the water there to explore the northern parts of the Park.

Figure 8. View of Edmonds-Kingston ferry terminal, from the park beach. Do not dive near the ferry.

Figure 9. Looking north from the jetty, along the beach. If you plan to explore the northern parts of the park, entering the water north of the jetty will save you a lot of air or surface swimming.

intended. If you also run low on air and have to surface swim against a tidal exchange, your return to shore could become very difficult. We've been there. Don't do it.

You know you're in trouble when...

We'll say it again—this place is big. If you're not sure where you are at anytime, you need to figure it out pronto. Don't dilly dally looking at things—figure out where you are! If you were dumb enough to go without a map, carefully surface and check your position relative to the shore features. If you have a map but can't figure out where you are on it, then you also should surface carefully to figure it out. Don't wait until you are low on air.

Marine Life

The fishing ban, combined with a lot of reef structure, has allowed the marine life to fluorish here. Large lingcod are the most striking life here, but there is some of just about everything.

shower head

Figure 10. Public restrooms and change rooms. The outdoor shower is turned off during the winter months.

Figure 11. Several informational signs describe various aspects of the park. Take time to peruse them.

buoys

Jetty Way trail starts here, at northern tip of jetty

Figure 12.
Left: view of the park buoys from the beach, south of the jetty.

below: View of park buoys from the tip of the jetty. Do not enter the water from the jetty—the rocks are slippery!

Surface buoys mark intersections of the underwater paths. Study them ahead of time.

tip of jetty

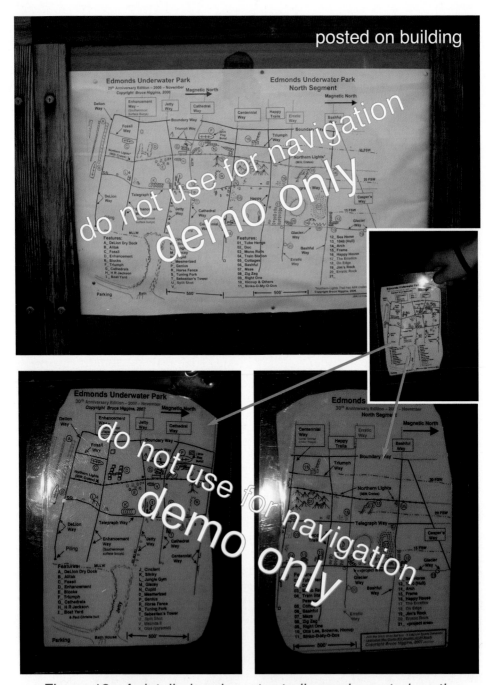

Figure 13. A detailed underwater trail map is posted on the facilities building. Two-sided plastic-coated copies are available at the Underwater Sports dive shop on Railroad Ave. Buy one and take it with you underwater. The site is constantly upgraded—make sure you have a current map!

Figure 14. This seaweed-obscured rope marks the start of Jetty Way at the northwest corner of the tip of the jetty. In the figure below the rope trail is visible looking down from the tip of the jetty at very low tide.

Figure 15. These pictures show a variety of trail markers used throughout Bruce Higins Underwater Trails Park.

The Paul Christie Hull
placed 2007

The Boatyard
18-28 feet depth
placed 1996

this teepee structure, near the
end of Jetty Way, is a twisted
lumber rack from Home Depot

concrete manhole collar
placed 1987

cairn
placed 2007

dive class landmark
placed 1996

8 feet diameter

Slinky
(sprinkler tubing)
18-28 feet depth
placed 1987

There are several bull kelp fields in the shallower parts of the park.

The Cathedrals are sections of concrete from repair and up-grade of the ferry ter-minal. They were placed in 1995 by Manson Construction for the city of Ed-monds.

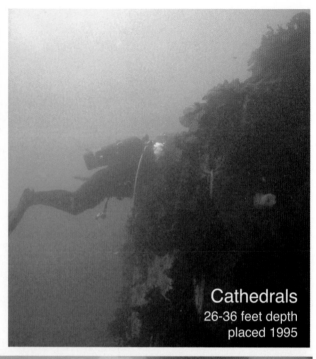

Cathedrals
26-36 feet depth
placed 1995

more of the Cathedrals

this giant earth mover tire is part of one
of the Cathedrals

Tube Henge

propellers from the
White Lightning

Tuning Fork
25-35 feet depth

Jungle Gym
18-28 feet depth'

The Passages

Enhancement
25-35 feet depth

pieces of Fossil
30-40 feet depth

Enhancement
25-35 feet depth

moon snail

moon snail

egg collar

123

kelp crabs hanging out on the path

lingcod in shallows

sunstar

dungeness crab claw

lingcod

squid eggs
10-20 feet depth

tube worm bouquet on Slinky
15-25 feet depth

Chanterelle
comfort food
316 Main Street
425 774 0650

Claire's Pantry
quality family dining
301 Main Street
425 776 2333

El Puerto
Mexican
423 Main Street
425 672 2469

Arnie's
high-end seafood, etc
300 Admiral Way
425 771 5688

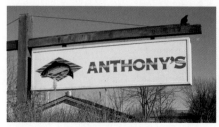

Anthony's
high-end seafood, etc
465 Admiral Way
425 771 4400

Some ways that the Bruce Higgins Underwater Trails dive site may change by the time you read this

This is a large, intensively maintained dive site Reef structure changes occur frequently. Take an up-to-date site map with you underwater.

Edmonds Marina Beach

(aka Edmonds Oil Dock)

Edmonds

There are two major diving attractions in Edmonds. Bruce Higgins Underwater Trails, next to the ferry terminal, gets the most attention. However, The Oil Dock at Edmonds Marina Beach is another worthwhile site, just a half mile south. Apart from full exposure to strong current at high flow times, this is a relatively easy dive, with a lot of marine life on old pilings. Don't worry about oil tankers— they stopped using this in the early 1990s. The dock site is being considered for a new ferry terminal, but the timing of that action may be years away. However, it is possible that the dock could be gone by the time you read this.

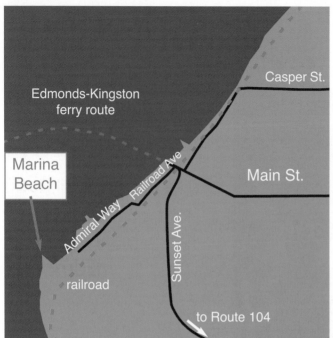

Figure 1. The Edmonds Oil Dock is on the Edmonds waterfront, two miles north of Seattle.

Figure 2. Aerial view of the Oil Dock in Edmonds Marine Park. (Photo from the Washington State Department of Ecology)

Getting there

Take the State Route 104 exit from I-5 and follow it down the the Edmonds Ferry Terminal. Pay attention as you drive down 104, because it does some twists and turns. When you get to the ferry terminal, turn left onto Railroad Ave. Follow it south and watch for signs for Edmonds Marina Beach (**Figure 1**). There are no signs announcing the oil dock, but it's hard to miss.

Parking

Parking is very convenient, and usually ample. Gear up at your car and walk to the beach, or carry your gear across the lawn to the beach and gear up there (**Figures 2 and 4**).

Amenities

Limited. Several porta-potties at the far end of the parking lot. No shower. The park itself is gorgeous, but the elaborate playground, picnic tables and large dog run won't be of interest to most divers (**Figure 3**).

Reef structure

The dock's pilings are *the* structure here! They hold a surprisingly large and varied amount of life (**Figures 7+**). The depth at the end of the dock is about 25-35 feet, depending on the tidal phase. The bottom drops off rapidly to either side of the pier. Only advanced divers should venture out of sight of the pilings.

Surface landmarks

The dock.

Swimming to the reef

We usually submerge as we walk out from the beach, staying within sight of the pilings. The visibility may not be great at the surface, but It usually improves 15-20 feet down. The best marine life and visibility starts at about two-thirds toward the end of the dock.

Currents

The oil dock is fully open to currents. Plan your dive to avoid strong tidal exchanges. If you choose to dive in a strong current, make sure to head back to shore with enough air to return along the bottom.

Figure 3. The park has a large well-equipped playground to the north of the pipeline and a large dog run to the south. This is a pretty good spot for non-divers to have some fun. The pipeline itself is non-functional and fenced off. Don't trespass.

end of dock

Figure 4. There's ample parking, very close to the water entry area.

Hazards
You are safe from boat traffic, as long as you stay under or near the pier. The current can be rough. It is a long way back from the end of the dock, so watch y ... air. Like any dive sites, it can be frightening to make a surface sw.. back to shore in a strong current.

You're in trouble when...
If you can't see at least one piling at all times, you are lost. Carefully surface and figure out how to get back under the dock.

.
Marine life
The area is a designated marine reserve. You won't see the numerous large lingcod that are so remarkable at Bruce Higgins Underwater Trails at the ferry terminal. But you may see just about anything here, depending on the day. The pilings are always full of invertebrates. Take your time to look at some of the more subtle life forms: sponges, barnacles, tube worms, etc. There is a massive collection of marine life under the end of the dock, but it is heavily shaded by the overhead dock and gets pretty dark. Bring a powerful flashlight.

enter water here

Figure 5. Southward view of the dock at the shoreline. Do not climb on the dock.

enter water here

Figure 6. View of the oil dock, looking out from the beach.

looking up

Figure 7. Most marine life at the Edmonds Oil dock is on the pilings. Take time to look for more subtle creatures.

full pilings

pilings
20-30 feet depth

brown sponge
20-30 feet depth

tube worms
21-31 feet depth

voracious sun star
25-35 feet depth

sun stars at end of dock
22-32 feet depth

you name it, it's here!

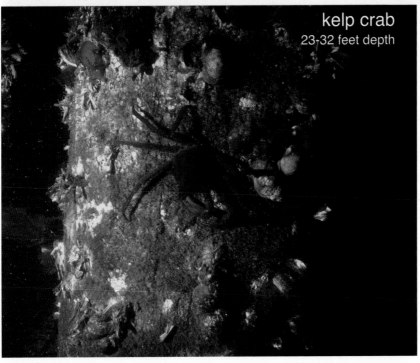

kelp crab
23-32 feet depth

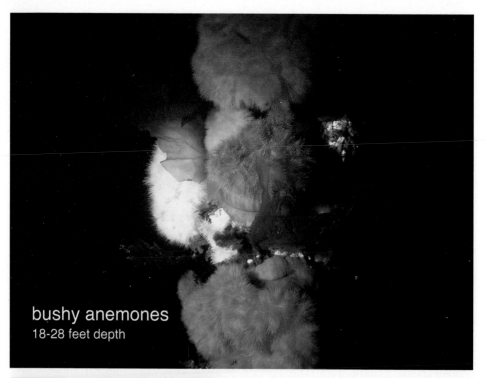

bushy anemones
18-28 feet depth

giant anemone
15-25 feet depth

blood star
10-20 feet depth

Anthony's
high end seafood, etc

465 Admiral Way
425 771 4400

Arnie's
high end seafood, etc

300 Admiral Way
425 771 5688

Anthony's and Arnies's seafood restaurants are less than a mile down Admiral Way. You can find many more restaurants on Main Street in Edmonds.

Some ways that the Marina Beach dive site may change by the time you read this

Plans to remove the dock are in the works. We pray that it does not happen in our lifetime. We are unaware of any plans to replace the dock with scuba-friendly structure.

The Junkyard at Alki

West Seattle

There are a number of sites around Puget Sound that might qualify as underwater junkyards. The one we are talking about here is a field of miscellaneous junk lying 20-60 feet underwater off the far south end of Alki Beach. Included are old plumbing fixtures, tires, cinder blocks, and miscellaneous metal pieces. Although some would call these underwater eyesores, they attract and support an interesting variety of marine life.

The Junkyard is a great place to start your shore diving experience. It is readily accessible, and the eclectic reef structures are fairly easy

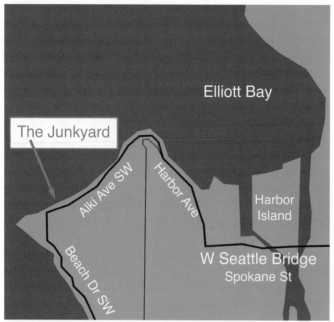

Figure 1. The Junkyard is at the south end of Alki Beach, on Alki Ave. SW.

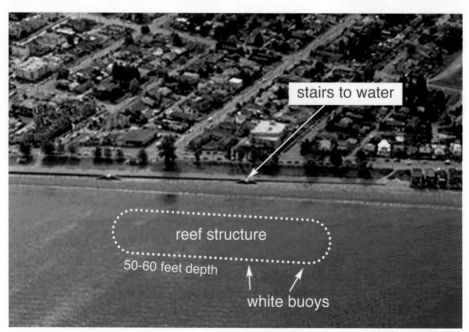

Figure 2. Aerial view of the Junkyard at Alki. The stairs make for easy entry to the beach. (Photo from the Washington State Department of Ecology)

to find. It's typically not as crowded with divers or beach goers as spots farther north on Alki.

Getting there
The Junkyard is on the south end of Alki Beach, in West Seattle. Take I-5 to the West Seattle Bridge and exit at Harbor Ave. Follow it 3.5 miles to the end of the beach, near the corner of 64th Ave SW and Alki Ave SW (**Figures 1 and 2**).

Parking
Parking is fairly convenient, provided you don't go on a weekend afternoon. With a little luck, you can park right in front of a set of stairs leading down to the beach (**Figures 3 and 4**). We usually gear up at our car and walk to the beach. If you get here on a crowded day, you can quickly unload your gear near the top of the stairs and then move your car a few blocks away from the beach.

Amenities
Nothing right there, but there are modern public bathrooms and an outdoor shower 0.2 miles to the east (**Figure 8**).

Reef structure
Most of the structure at the Junkyard is along guide ropes that run parallel to the beach (**Figures**). The piles of miscellaneous junk are amusing to explore, and attract a variety of fish and crustaceans.

Surface landmarks
The most important landmark at the Junkyard is the line of white buoys anchored at a depth of about 45 feet, parallel to the beach. We usually swim out from the stairs, perpendicular to the beach, and head right or left along the junk fields.

Swimming to the reef
Enter the water by walking down the concrete stairs to the beach. You can see several white buoys that warn boats to stay away (**Figures 9 and 10**). The drop-off is rapid, so surface swimming is not really called for.

Currents
Alki point affords some protection from currents, but they can be

Figure 3. There is usually street parking available just up from the beach, except on sunny weekends.

Figure 4. Looking down the stairs to the beach. Most divers gear up at their cars and walk down the stairs in their gear.

southwest view

northeast view

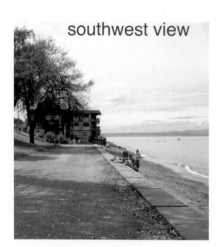
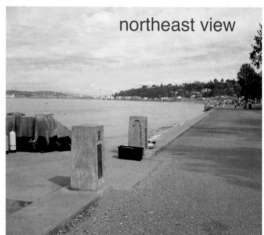

Figure 5. Looking southwest and northeast along the seawall. Even on a weekend, it is relatively quiet down here compared to the main drag farther north.

strong at times of high tidal exchange.

Hazards
Watch out for kayakers and small motorized craft. There are occasional crabbers around.

You know you're in trouble when...
If you are deeper than 60 feet, you are too far from shore.

Marine life
Larger fish and crabs are scarce, but there are lots of more subtle creatures. Mostly crustaceans and small fish. Look carefully in the wide eel grass beds for unusual crabs and nudibranchs. This area is *not* a marine preserve—we hope the city makes it one in the future.

Figure 6. View of top of stairs, from promenade.

Figure 7. At low tide, the stairs lead down to the beach. At high tide, the water covers the lower stairs.

Figure 8. These public bathrooms and shower are located 0.2 miles east on Alki Ave SW.

white buoy

buoy block
45 feet MLLW

Figure 9. This is the view from the breakwall looking west. The white buoys run at about 45 feet depth, just beyond most of the junk. That's Bainbridge Island in the distance.

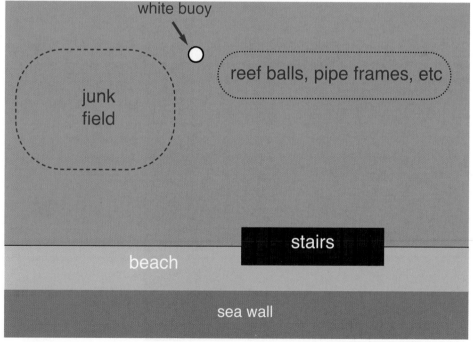

white buoy

junk field

reef balls, pipe frames, etc

stairs

beach

sea wall

Figure 10. Schematic of reef structure layout. There are underwater guide ropes running through the reefs, but we can't guarantee they will still be there by the time you read this.

sandy bottom
10-20 feet depth

Figure 11. You'll pass sand, eelgrass and sand again on your way out to the structures at 40 feet depth.

miscellaneous junk
35-45 feet depth

bathtub
35-45 feet depth

Figure 12. The pictures on this page were taken in the junkfields to the south of the white buoys.

PVC sculpture
40-50 feet depth

broken piling
25-35 feet depth

another junkpile
35-45 feet depth

The pictures on this page were all taken north of the stairs at about 40 feet depth. They give you an idea of the size and layout of some of the structure. (A flash doesn't help much when taking photos at these distances from the subjects.)

guide rope

photo taken with flash

guide rope

reef balls
40-50 feet depth

reef balls
taken with flash

hermit crab
4-14 feet depth

canary rockfish
35-45 feet depth

ratfish
20-30 feet depth

tube dwelling anemone
12-22 feet depth

crab trap
35-45 feet depth

153

red flabellina
(nudibranch)
20-30 feet depth

diver's finger

quilback rockfish
30-40 feet depth

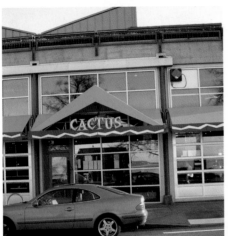

Cactus
high end Tex-Mex

2820 Alki Ave SW
206 933 6000

Pegasus
well-executed pizza, etc

2758 Alki Ave SW
206 932 4849

Spud fish and chips
good at what they do

2666 Alki Ave SW
206 938 5119

Some ways that the Junkyard dive site may change by the time you read this

This is an unofficial dive site, maintained by an informal group of individuals and clubs. Changes to the rope trails and reef structures occur sporadically and unpredictably.

Les Davis Marine Park

Tacoma

1940

L es Davis Marine Park is located along Ruston Way, an idyllic stretch of Tacoma waterfront. This is a great route for walking, biking, roller-blading, eating and scuba-diving (**Figure 3**). It is the centerpiece of some very well-executed urban redevelopment.

Les Davis Marine Park is a newer dive site, comprised of concrete pieces from the Tacoma Narrows Bridge (Galloping Gertie) that collapsed in 1940. This is an easy dive, enhanced by a set of stairs leading from the walkway to a diver-friendly mini cove. The cove's pebble bottom is an ideal place to make final gear adjustments before

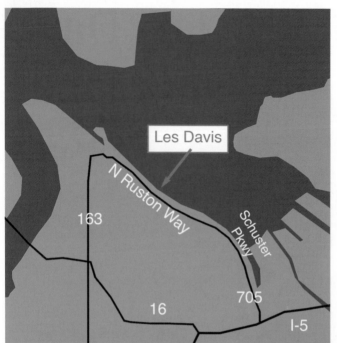

Figure 1. Les Davis Marine Park is in the center of the Ruston Way waterfront walkway.

Figure 2. Aerial view of Les Davis Marine Park. (Photo from the Washington State Department of Ecology)

heading for deeper water. Thank the Washington Scuba Alliance for spear-heading the stair installation.

This spot has relatively mild currents. It is generally considered safe for all levels of dive expertise. It is also a popular certification spot. Visibility is more varied here than at most other sites, partly due to the Puyallup River emptying into the Sound to the east.

Getting there
Take Interstate 705 west from I-5. Follow it to Schuster Parkway and then follow signs for Ruston Way (**Figure 1**). Jack Hyde Park at Commencement Bay is the first formal park area on Ruston Way. About a quarter mile further west is Les Davis Marine Park. Park by the fishing pier, about 50 yards from the dive entry (**Figures 3-5**).

Parking
There is ample parking, even on most weekends (**Figures 2 and 4**). We usually gear up at our car and walk to the dive steps. Some divers carry their gear to picnic tables near the entry stairs (**Figure 6**).

Amenities
Public bathrooms at the fishing pier (**Figure 4**). No shower or change rooms. There are many good restaurants on Ruston Way, within a 10 minute walk of the dive site.

Reef structure
The major reef attraction is a line of concrete bridge debris from Galloping Gertie. The bottom drops off quickly, so you don't have to get far from shore to see the reef structure, which includes an earthmover tire and a fish sculpture out from the dive stairs (**Figure 7**). The line of tumbled concrete runs parallel to shore and makes for some eerie sights (**Figure 8**). You should see parts of it when you get to about 30-40 feet depth, swimming out perpendicular from shore. Follow it to its end to your left (west) or a limited distance to the east. Stop when you see the tire reef, as you will be getting close to the fishing pier (**Figure 9**). Bring a flashlight to explore nooks and crannies for octos (**Figure 8**).

Figure 3. This section of Ruston Way has some interesting city landmarks. When not diving on a scuba outing, we bicycle along here to take in the sights.

Ruston Way

parking lot

public bathrooms

LES DAVIS PIER

dive stairs

Figure 4. View from parking lot, looking west towards the dive entrance. The walk from the parking lot to the stairs is a little long, but manageable.

Surface landmarks

There are no surface landmarks for the reef itself. The set of buoys that you can see from shore are farther out than you should be diving. Did we tell you to stay away from the pier?

Swimming to the reef

Walk straight down the entry stairs and make final gear adjustments in the shallow cove. From there, head straight out from the beach. The reef structure should be obvious once you get to about 40-50 feet depth. The fish sculpture in Figure 7 is located at a depth of about 25-35 feet depth, at the shoreside edge of the reef. It is just to the east of the dive entry stairs.

Currents

Les Davis is deep inside Commencement Bay, which provides protection from tidal flows. The currents are relatively mild here.

Hazards

Make sure you know where the pier is and stay away from it. You run the risk of getting tangled in old line. Fisherpeople get irritated with divers in their territory. They have been known to call the police to cite offending divers! Be wary of boats. Use a dive flag.

You know you're in trouble when...

The highlights of this site are the concrete bridge debris. If you are more than 40 feet down, you should be able to see debris at all times. If not, go shallower and surface to get your bearings.

Marine life

This site does not have as much marine life as some other sites, but you can still see just about anything here, depending on the day. There are more nudibranchs in the shallows here than we've seen anywhere else.

Figure 5. The fishing pier pilings are loaded with life. **Don't** dive there to check it out! You can see similar stuff safely at the dive site.

Figure 6. The dive stairs offer an easy walk down to a small pebble beach, a perfect place to double check gear before submerging.

dive stairs

fishing pier in distance

this small cove makes for a great entry site

dive stairs

earthmover tire

Figure 7. Head out at about 30° from the dive stairs to find the large tire and the fish sculpture.

fish sculpture
approximately 25-35 feet depth

Galloping Gertie debris
35-45 feet depth

Figure 8. Some of the bridge debris at shallower parts of the reef.

more bridge debris
35-45 feet depth

These green pictures were taken at about 60 feet depth, without a flash.

pile of concrete slabs
55-65 feet depth

a flashlight is helpful here
50-60 feet depth

tire bundle (large)

65-75 feet depth

Figure 9. Scattered tire bundles at the eastern end of the dive site. There are also some scattered unbundled tires in the concrete debris in this area. The picture quality is poor due to depth, but it is important that you know that these are a warning sign that you are getting close to the the pier!

Very important

You will see scattered tire bundles as you approach the fishing pier. Do not swim further east toward the pier—you risk getting tangled in fishing line.

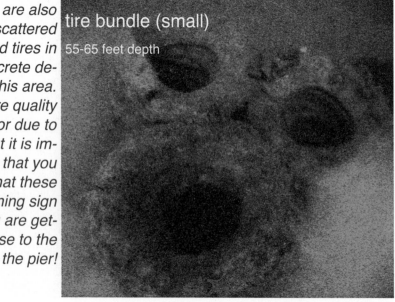

tire bundle (small)

55-65 feet depth

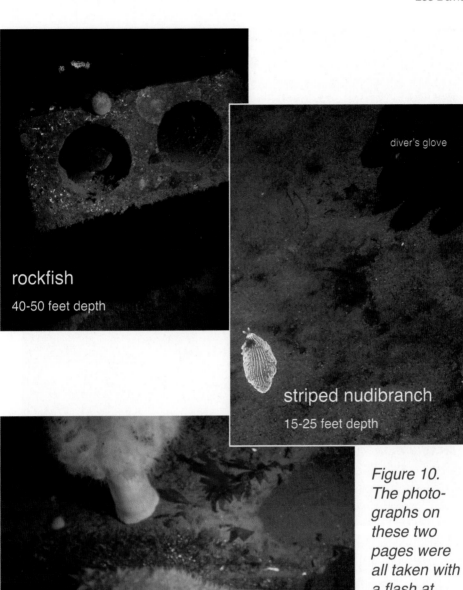

rockfish

40-50 feet depth

diver's glove

striped nudibranch

15-25 feet depth

California sea cucumber

60-70 feet depth

Figure 10. The photographs on these two pages were all taken with a flash at close range.

white-lined dirona nudibranch
60-70 feet depth

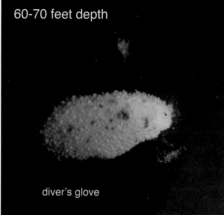

60-70 feet depth

diver's glove

plumose anemones
60-70 feet depth

vermillion star
60-70 feet depth

black-clawed crab(?)

C.I. Shenanigans
high-end everything

3017 Ruston Way
253 752 8811

Katie Downs
fancy casual variety food

3211 Ruston Way
253 756 0771

Duke's Chowder House
classic casual seafood

3327 Ruston Way
253 752 5444

RAM Restaurant & Brewery
casual everything and beer

3001 Ruston Way
253 756 7886

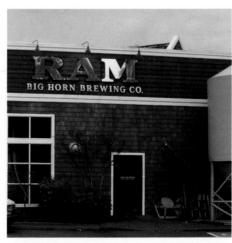

Some ways that the Les Davis dive site may change by the time you read this

We are unaware of planned changes to the site.

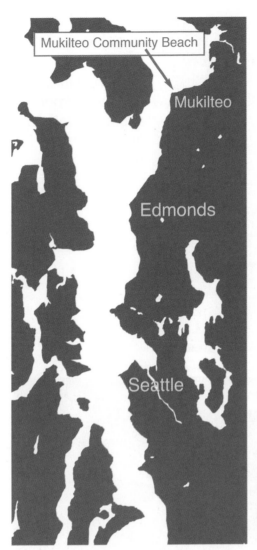

Mukilteo Community Beach

Mukilteo Community Beach

Mukilteo

There is one informal dive site near the Mukilteo ferry terminal. Diving takes place from Mukilteo Community Beach Park, immediately west of the NOAA T-dock. This site is readily accessible via a short set of stairs between the NOAA station and the Silver Cloud Inn (**Figure 4**). There is no local search and rescue capacity at this site. Divers use the waters at their own risk.

Older publications describe two additional Mukilteo shore dive sites: Mukilteo Lighthouse Park (formerly Lighthouse State Park) and the old Air Force oil dock. In 2008, the city of Mukilteo outlawed shore

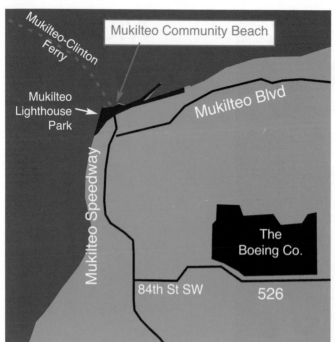

Figure 1. The Mukilteo dive site is on the Mukilteo ferry waterfront, approximately 25 miles north of Seattle.

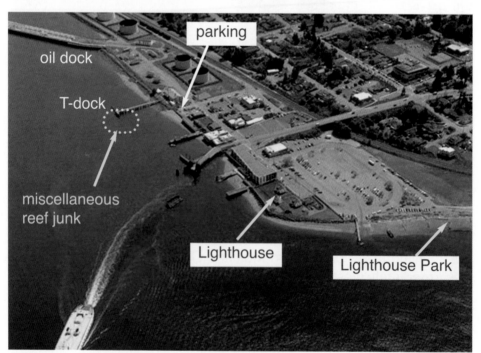

Figure 2. Aerial view of the three potential dive spots at Mukilteo. (Photo from the Washington State Department of Ecology)

diving from Mukilteo Lighthouse Park due to safety concerns related to the adjacent boat launch. The offshore region of the park is now legally accessible to divers only by boat.

The other potential Mukilteo dive spot is the deteriorating Air Force oil dock, east of Community Beach (**Figure 2**). The dock topside and the tank farm is off limits to divers, so getting to it from shore requires a long swim from Community Beach. The oil dock will probably be removed in the future. It is being considered for a new ferry terminal site. There are also environmental concerns about its creosote-treated pilings.

Although you may read some glowing descriptions of Mukilteo's Community Beach dive site, this is not one or our fa-

> # Announcement
>
> Due to diver complaints regarding disruption of the Community Beach dive site by group dives, the City now requires that formal parties of 5 or more (this means certification and training groups) obtain a Special Event Permit from the Recreational and Cultural Services Division of The City of Mukilteo. See the City of Mukilteo website for details.

vorites. It is over-dived and fairly barren, and most of the discarded objects you'll encounter are not pretty. Furthermore, this place took a big hit in 2005 when the older wooden T-dock pilings were replaced with concrete ones. Removing the wood pilings cleaned out most of the marine life that clung to them. Fortunately, marine life is re-building on the new pilings.

Another important point about this site is that it is heavily used for diving certification classes and advanced training. Be prepared for crowds if your timing is bad. We stay away on weekends and holidays, even during the winter.

Okay, okay, enough with the negative and cautionary statements. We do like this place, have dived it several times and will be back. On a very positive note, there is the potential to make this a *great* dive site by adding some environmentally friendly reef structure and designating it a marine stewardship area. With relatively little effort, the dive community and city and state leaders could work together to turn this place into a Puget Sound scuba jewel.

ferry boarding ramp

Lighthouse Park

T-Dock

Mukilteo Lighthouse Park

The Mukilteo ferry
from the Silver Cloud balcony

Figure 3. The Mukilteo ferry terminal is the center of a bustling collection of shops, restaurants, parkland and government facilities.

Getting there

The simplest way to get here from Seattle is to take I-5 exit 182 in Lynnwood and head north on SR 525 (Mukilteo Speedway). Follow the signs to the ferry terminal, and take a right just before the boarding area (**Figures 1 and 3**).

Parking

There are several parking spaces at the Community Beach lot (**Figure 4**). Additional parking is available south of the Park, and at Lighthouse Park. Don't use the covered hotel parking.

Amenities

Public bathrooms are available at Lighthouse Park. Don't use the hotel facilities—previous divers already gave us a bad rep with hotel management, who have otherwise been very gracious. No on-site shower.

Reef structure

The reef structure includes the concrete T-dock pilings, with a moderate amount of marine life. There is an eclectic, junky collection of stuff just to the west of the T-dock. The most talked-about is a large (20') geodome made from PVC pipe (**Figure 9**). Miscellaneous plumbing fixtures, old tires, fire hydrants, pilings, etc are scattered around.

Apart from the T-dock pilings, your best chance to see interesting marine life is to swim east toward the oil dock to explore the miscellaneous old pilings and discarded items between the T-dock and the oil dock, at approximately 10 to 60 feet depth.

Surface landmarks

The concrete pilings of the T-dock are your surface markers. The only diver-specific landmarks *may* be buoys west of the T-dock (**Figure 6**). The geodome has been marked by a buoy at times. These markers could easily be different by the time you read this. In fact, they were missing when we dove the site in September, 2008. We have not been able to figure out who is making the changes. Be prepared for something other than what you read here.

stairs to beach

Figure 4. There are several parking spots right at the beach entry, with more close by. Don't park in the covered hotel spots.

Swimming to the reef
Enter at the west side of the T-dock and descend along the pilings. The sand/gravel bottom drops off rapidly. Pick a depth between 10 and 60 feet and head west to explore. If you want to see it all, sweep east and west at different depths.

The oil dock is officially off-limits to divers. The only way to get there is to swim from the western T-dock entry site. The distance is doable, but preferably as a surface swim near shore, in order to conserve air. Walking there along the beach with your gear is a possibility that we have not tried.

Currents
Moderate, due to Mukilteo Lighthouse Park headlands.

Hazards
There is boat traffic in and around this area, as well as fishing nets and crab pots. A dive flag is a good idea, especially if you are venturing away from the T-dock.

You're in trouble when...
Watch your depth. The steep, sandy bottom makes it very easy to descend past 60 feet without realizing it. And the lack of reef structure will make you want to go deeper to see more. Resist the temptation unless you are properly trained.

Marine life
With the risk of sounding overly negative, we will say it again—this is not a great place for marine life. It is quite barren. Night divers have a better chance of seeing remarkable creatures.

Figure 5. This is the waterside view looking back toward the parking lot. The parking and gear-up area is extremely convenient, as long as you do not come on a nice weather weekend.

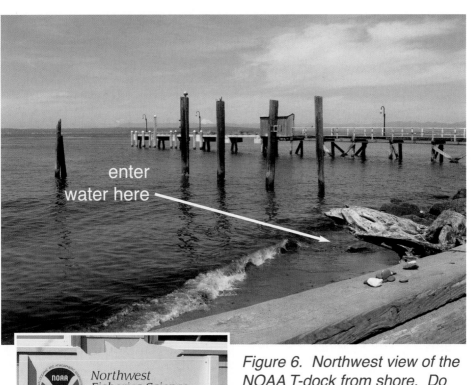

enter
water here

Northwest
Fisheries Science
Center
**Mukilteo
Research
Station**
10 Park Avenue, Building B

*Figure 6. Northwest view of the
NOAA T-dock from shore. Do
not climb on the dock.*

tip of NOAA
T-dock

you may see marker
buoys here, but they
change frequently

oil dock

Figure 7. The oil dock is owned by the Air Force, but may be turned over to the Port of Everett. The dock itself is in disrepair. It is still unclear how the site will be used. Entry here is not authorized

NO TRESPASSING
US GOVERNMENT PROPERTY
WARNING
AUTHORIZED PERSONNEL ONLY
AREA UNDER SURVEILLANCE

IT IS UNLAWFUL TO ENTER THIS AREA WITHOUT PERMISSION
FROM NOAA. ALL PERSONNEL AND THE PROPERTY UNDER
THEIR CONTROL WITHIN THIS AREA ARE SUBJECT TO SEARCH.

41 CFR Subpart 101-20.3 Conduct on Federal Property.

EXPLOSIVES, FIREARMS, ALCOHOLIC BEVERAGES, AND ILLEGAL
DRUGS ARE PROHIBITED.

oil dock deck

Mukilteo

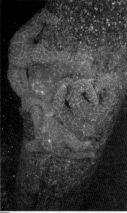

Figure 8. The
T-dock pilings
host a variety
of marine life.

25-35 feet depth

12-22 feet depth

55-65 feet depth

Figure 9. This 20-foot diameter PVC pipe geodome is the most talked-about structure here. It is an imposing sight at about 55 feet MLLW, just west and deep to the T-dock.

This 2-foot statue stands inside the base of the geodome (Sept, 08).

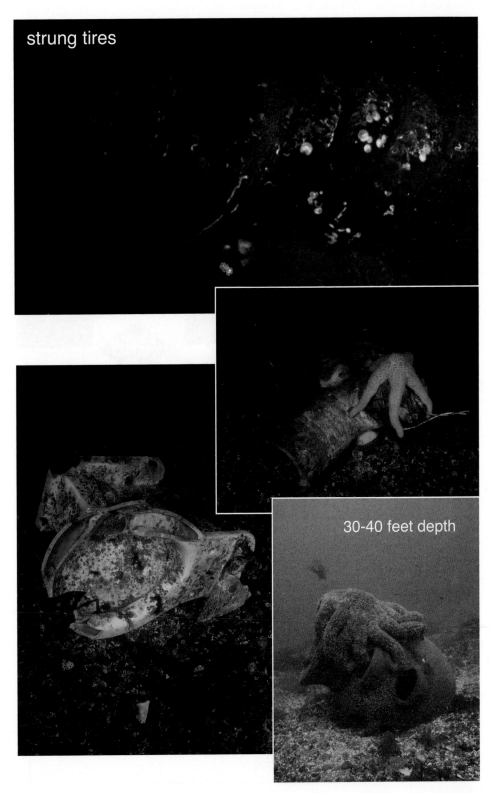

strung tires

30-40 feet depth

Ivar's
high end seafood, etc

on the water—great views
710 Front St
425 742 6180

Arnie's
high end seafood, etc

just up the hill
714 2nd St
425 355 2181

Some ways that the Mukilteo dive site may change by the time you read this

1. The old oil dock to the east of Community Beach is likely to be removed.

2. The surface markers and reef structure just west of the T-dock are not officially maintained. Anything could happen—removal, movement, or additions.

Redondo Beach

Des Moines

Redondo Beach is a very popular seaside recreational area in Des Moines. It has become an increasingly popular dive site, with an eclectic variety of structures placed along thick guide ropes, at 35-70 feet depth. These reef structures range from the typical tires and pipes to the more bizarre—rocking horses, plastic skulls and PVC pipe artwork. Guide ropes and moderate currents make it fairly easy to explore the reef structures. Typically it's not crowded here, except on weekends.

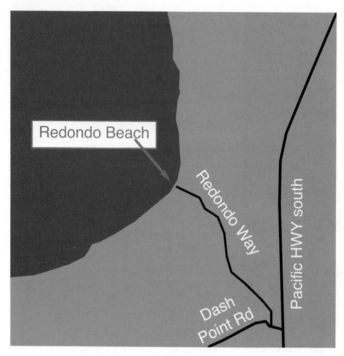

Figure 1. Redondo is about 12 miles south of Seattle.

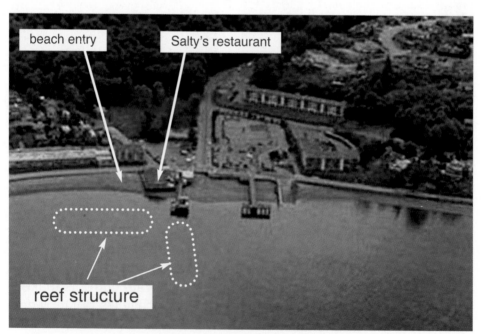

Figure 2. Aerial view of the Redondo site. (Photo from the Washington State Department of Ecology)

Getting there

Redondo is on the west side of Puget Sound, 12 miles south of Seattle. Take exit 143 from I-5, and go west on S 329th street to Hwy 99. Go south on Pacific Highway South to Dash Point Way (route 509) Turn right on Dash Point Road and take another right at Redondo Way, which takes you directly down to the beach.

Parking

There are several parking spaces right next to the beach, but you need to be early or lucky to get one. Otherwise, you can park and gear up at the larger public lot across the street, and walk to the water in your gear. Local residents (and the police) get pretty cranked up over divers parking illegally along the beach, so don't do it. We usually drop our stuff off at the beach, park the car a couple of blocks away, and then return to gear up on the wall that separates the sidewalk from the beach.

Amenities

It's all here. Showers, bathrooms, parking and a comfortable beach. And a very good restaurant.

Reef structure

Most of the structure at Redondo is along guide ropes that run parallel to the beach north of Salty's, and perpendicularly out from the northeast corner of Salty's. The north end of one rope is hooked to a submerged Volkswagen (September, 2008). Near the ropes is an eclectic collection of items, including a stove, PVC structures, and stacked highway reflectors.

The variety of reef structure placed here ranges from eco-friendly (stone wall) to the bizarre (a rocking horse on a sunken boat). Some divers will be amused by the wide variety of underwater junk here. Others will be disgusted.

Surface landmarks

The most important surface landmark at Redondo Beach is Salty's restaurant. An assortment of large structures runs north, parallel to the beach from the north corner of the restaurant. A second collection of reef structure is scattered west, perpendicular to the beach from

north

Figure 3.
There are a few
parking spots
adjacent to the
beach. But you
have to be
early or lucky to
get one.

Figure 4. There is a
large parking lot across
the street from Salty's.
Ample sidestreet parking
can be found within a few
blocks of the water.

north

Figure 5. Look-
ing north from
the site, along
the Puget
Sound shore-
line.

the north corner of the restaurant. Don't dive to the south of Salty's, near the boat launch or piers.

Swimming to the reef

The rope and reef structures are close enough to the beach that surface swimming is unnecessary. We usually submerge as we walk out from the beach, and head out perpendicular to the beach until we find the guide rope.

Currents

Redondo is inside Poverty Bay, which acts to moderate current flows here.

Hazards

Watch out for watercraft. The boat ramp and dock south of Salty's restaurant are heavily used. There may be a buoy to mark Redondo as a dive site.

> ## Important
>
> There is some friction between divers and the many other users of this beach. We have to be considerate, or risk having the city curtail our use.

Use a dive flag, especially if you plan to look for debris in front of Salty's.

Marine life

This is not a great place for marine life. It is not a marine preserve. The area is heavily fished from boats and the nearby pier. You'll see mostly crustaceans and smaller fish.

Figure 6. At low tide, Salty's pier is completely exposed.

Figure 7. Don't dive by the city fishing pier, south of the site.

Figure 8. Stay away from the public boat launch.

Figure 9. There are public showers on the south side of the public bathroom, on the city pier south of Salty's. Showers are great, but they are a bit of a trek from the dive site.

Figure 10. View from beach, as you enter the water. There was no surface buoy at the site at the time this picture was taken. The corner of Salty's is your best above-water marker.

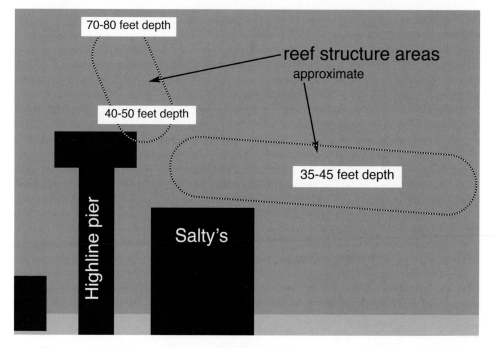

Figure 11. The reef structure is directly out west and north of Salty's.

guide rope

guide rope

This VW is north of Salty's, at the north end of the thick guiderope.

PVC pipe boat
30-40 feet depth

Figure 12. Most of the structures on these two pages are to the north of Salty's, on or near a thick guide rope.

large pipe

stone wall
40-50 feet depth

stacked highway
reflectors
40-50 feet depth

guide rope

guide rope

sunken motor boat

horse
photographed
with flash

guide rope

Figure 13. The structures on these two pages are scattered westward from the north corner of Salty's. Be careful going southward because you will get into heavier boat traffic, and you can get pretty far from shore. It's a good idea to return to shore along the bottom, so watch your air supply!

lingcod on stove
35-45 feet depth

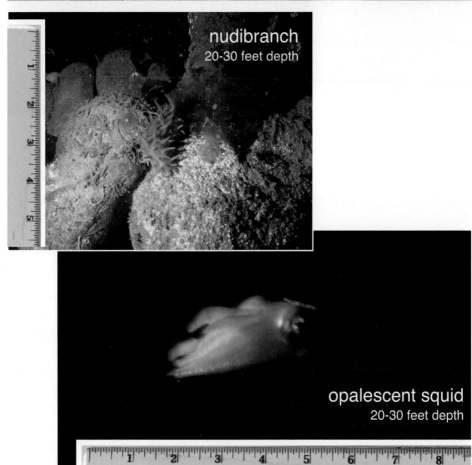

nudibranch
20-30 feet depth

opalescent squid
20-30 feet depth

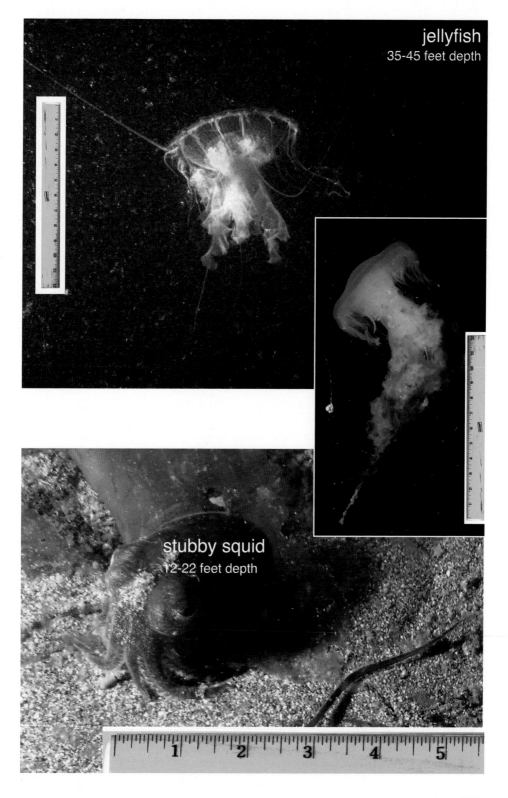

jellyfish
35-45 feet depth

stubby squid
12-22 feet depth

Salty's at Redondo Beach
high-end seafood
28201 Redondo Beach Drive South
253 272 0607

Some ways that the Redondo dive site may change by the time you read this

This is an unofficial "wild west" dive site, maintained by an informal group of individuals and clubs. Changes to the rope trails and reef structures occur sporadically and unpredictably. Nothing would surprise us here!

Saltwater State Park

Des Moines

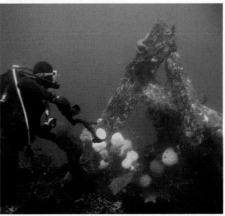

S altwater State Park, opened in 1926, includes 88 acres of land and more than 1,400 feet of shoreline. The beach and park facilities are heavily used by non-divers. The reef structure was originally placed in the 1970s, under the direction of the Washington State Parks and Recreation Commission. McSorley Creek, a salmon spawning habitat, enhances the variety of marine life here.

Saltwater is one of the best dive sites near Seattle. We are surprised at how few divers we see here, and consider it one of the better-kept scuba secrets. One of the reasons for its underuse is the relatively

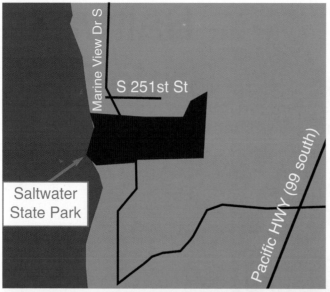

Figure 1. Saltwater State Park is in the city of Des Moines, about 9 miles south of Seattle.

Figure 2. This aerial view of the park shows how McSorley Creek enters Puget Sound at the dive site. The distance from the water's edge to the reef structure varies substantially with the tide. (Photo from the Washington State Department of Ecology)

long swim to the reef structure. But don't let that stop you from seeing this place. Just be mindful of the technical issues described below.

Saltwater is scheduled to undergo a major upgrade in 2009. A substantial amount of rock and concrete reef structure is to be added at the periphery of the current structure. If carried out as planned, this place will go from very good to awesome.

Getting there
Saltwater State Park is in Des Moines, 9 miles south of Seattle. Take I-5 exit 149 and follow the S Kent Des Moines Rd (Highway 516) west past Highway 99 South, to Marine View Drive. Follow Marine View south about 1.4 miles. There should be a sign at South 251st street directing you into the park entrance (**Figure 1**).

Parking
A large parking lot serves all users of the park (**Figure 3**). Parking is fairly convenient, provided you don't go on a weekend afternoon. With a little luck, you can snag one of several spots right in front of the beach. We usually gear up at our car and walk to the beach.

Amenities
This place has it all. Convenient parking, a shower, modern spacious bathrooms and a snack cafe (**Figures 4 and 12**).

Reef structure
Most of the structure at Saltwater is along a bundle of guide cables that runs parallel to the beach (**Figures 5, 6 and 9**). At the north end of the cable trail is what's left of a sunken barge (**Figures 6, 8 and 10**). At the south end is a tepee structure made of concrete beams (**Figures 6 and 11**). Between the barge and the tepee are scattered tires and miscellaneous concrete debris which host a large variety of marine life. The concrete structures are usually teeming with fish. The discarded tires, like tire reefs elsewhere, have not worked out so well.

Swimming to the reef structure
Gear up and walk straight down the paths, from the parking lot to the beach. You should see a white and red buoy that marks the sunken barge at the north end of the reef structure (**Figures 6 and 7**). The

Figure 3. There is a large parking lot at the beach. This is a marine protected area. Removal of any marine life or artifact is not permitted.

path to beach

buoy looks far away when standing on shore, especially at high tide, since the beach is very flat where McSorley Creek enters. A row of flimsy posts mark the southern park boundary, which extends out perpendicular from the beach just south of the reef structure (**Figure 7**).

To get to the reef structure, take a compass reading just to the left of the red and white buoy. Submerge as you walk out from the beach, and follow your reading until you find the guide cables at about 20-30 feet depth, depending on the tidal phase.

We prefer to wade out and submerge once the water is a few feet deep. There is a lot of marine life even in the shallows on the way out. Alternatively, you may prefer to surface swim to the buoy that marks the sunken barge and then follow its line down. However, it is a relatively long surface swim. And descending down a buoy line in soupy surface conditions can be a little unnerving.

Currents
Saltwater is fully exposed to current, with minimal headlands in the area. Although the current seems to run purely parallel to shore, it is definitely more pleasant to dive here during slack. Even a mild current can be problematic if you are far from shore, tired and low on air.

Hazards
Watch out for boats. A dive flag is a good idea. Be careful not to get snagged on metal spikes sticking up from the barge (**Figure 10**). Make sure to reserve enough air so that you can swim back along the bottom, avoiding the currents. Did we mention that the reef structure is relatively far from shore?

You know you are in trouble when...
All of the reef structure here is in less than 70 feet of water. If you are 60 feet or deeper and have not found the cable trail, you have missed it. This could happen if you get off course on your way out to the reef. Getting further from shore than the reef structure could put you in scuba jeopardy. If you cannot quickly figure out your mistake and re-orient, you need to surface and look for the can buoy. If you cannot see it, get to it safely, or quickly re-orient yourself, return to shore.

McSorley Creek

Figure 4. McSorley Creek is being rehabilitated as a salmon spawning area.

SPECIAL NOTICE
CONSUMING ALCOHOL OR
POSSESSING OPEN ALCOHOLIC
BEVERAGE CONTAINERS
PROHIBITED IN
SALTWATER STATE PARK

playgrounds, picnic tables, bathrooms

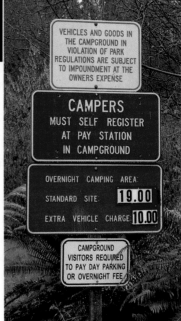

VEHICLES AND GOODS IN
THE CAMPGROUND IN
VIOLATION OF PARK
REGULATIONS ARE SUBJECT
TO IMPOUNDMENT AT THE
OWNERS EXPENSE

CAMPERS
MUST SELF REGISTER
AT PAY STATION
IN CAMPGROUND

OVERNIGHT CAMPING AREA
STANDARD SITE: 19.00
EXTRA VEHICLE CHARGE: 10.00

CAMPGROUND
VISITORS REQUIRED
TO PAY DAY PARKING
OR OVERNIGHT FEE

reef structure
along cables

red and white can buoy

Maurey Island

Figure 5. View from beach, as you enter the water. A red and white can buoy marks the sunken barge (9/08). To the left is a row of plastic posts, which are not visible in this photo.

Marine life

We typically see a rich variety of marine life here. There seems to be more small and medium size fish than at any other site described in this book.

> **Very important**
> *The marker cables at this site can be hidden by seaweed overgrowth, depending on the season and the degree of site maintenance.*

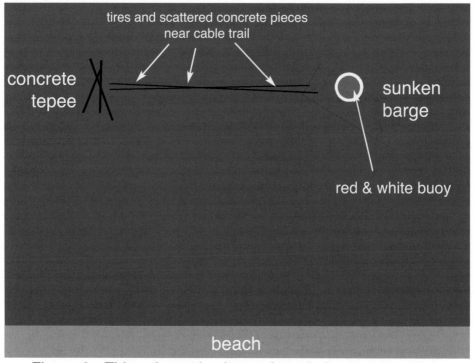

concrete tepee

tires and scattered concrete pieces near cable trail

sunken barge

red & white buoy

beach

Figure 6. This schematic shows the relative location of the sunken barge and the concrete tepee, the structures that mark the north and south ends of the reef structure. This rough sketch is not drawn accurately to scale!

Figure 7. These plastic posts mark the south end of the park, which abuts private waterfront. Don't trespass. We suspect that these markers will be replaced with something more substantial with the upcoming park upgrade.

Figure 8. This photo shows the red and white can buoy line at-tached to a piece of the sunken barge deck. We're showing you this because the barge is in an advanced state of decay, and you may not even recognize it as a barge when you see it. And remember, this scene may change with the future park upgrade.

Figure 9. These photos of the underwater marker cables were taken several months apart. In that time, seaweed has obscured them. As at other dive sites, you need to remember that things can appear very different from season-to-season, and depending on whether the site has been maintained.

207

Figure 10. The barge lies on a slope, from 30-40 feet depth, depending on the tidal phase. It blends in with the ocean floor, and may not be readily apparent to you. These metal pieces pro-trude from the deck. Be careful not to snag your equipment!

concrete tepee
22-32 feet depth

concrete stack
23-33 feet depth

Figure 11. There is a variety of large concrete pieces, mostly at the southern end of the site. These attract a lot of fish.

concrete block

section of tire reef

anemones on tire
23-33 feet depth

10-20 feet depth

squid eggs
12-22 feet depth

skate
10-20 feet depth

Figure 12. The cafe has indoor seating. It is open year-round.

Some ways that the Saltwater dive site may change by the time you read this

This site is scheduled for a major upgrade in the very near future. Substantial rock and concrete formations are to be added to the periphery of the existing reef structure. Doing so should elevate this place from very good to awesome. However, before diving this site, it is important that you check with dive resources for more up-to-date information about how the layout changes from what is described here. Start with your local dive shop, the Des Moines Parks and Recreation, and the Washington State Parks and Recreation web sites. Many of the local scuba websites will undoubtedly describe the coming changes as time goes on.

October, 2008

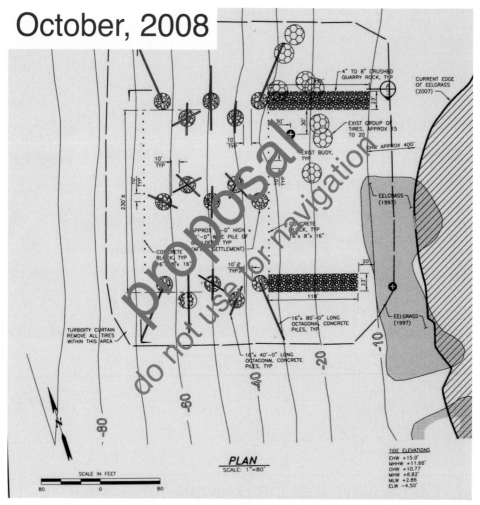

Seacrest

Cove 1
Cove 2
Cove 3

Seattle

S eacrest Park is one of the most popular Puget Sound dive spots. It's a prime certification site, with some interesting structures and marine life. It also has all of the amenities we could ask for—bathrooms, changing rooms, a shower and restaurants. Thank the Seattle City Council and numerous dedicated dive advocates for making this a scuba playland. It is surprising and encouraging that the marine life survives the heavy recreational use of the area.

Showing up at Seacrest on a weekend is like going to a block party. Combine the certification classes with the experienced divers there

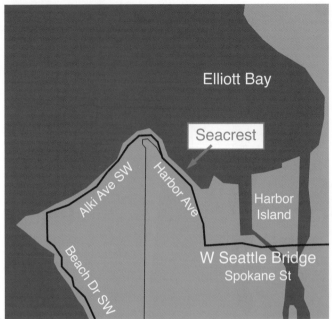

Figure 1. Seacrest Park is on Elliott bay, in West Seattle.

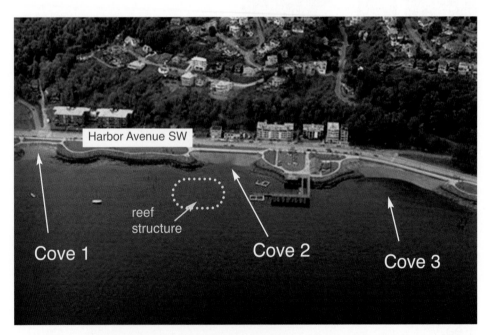

Figure 2. Aerial view of Seacrest Park. Cove 2 is where you'll find most of the marine life, structure and humans. (Photo from the Washington State Department of Ecology).

Figure 3. Seacrest has a lot to offer beginning and advanced divers, but brace yourself for a lot of company!

for the scenery, and it can get pretty crowded (**Figure 3**). Even in the middle of winter during a cold rain, there can be a surprising number of divers here. We avoid this place on weekends.

Getting there
From I-5, take the West Seattle Bridge. Get off at the Harbor Ave exit (**Figure 1**). Seacrest is about 1.5 miles down Harbor Ave, just past Salty's Restaurant.

Parking
There is ample street parking, along with 20+ spaces at the water taxi dock. Finding a spot is no problem during the week, but you'd better be early or lucky on a sunny weekend. We usually gear up at our car

Figure 4. Each of the three coves has its own distinct lay-out. Most of the scuba action is at Cove 2. The city and the dive community are talking about ways to enhance Coves 1 and 3 for scuba.

Figure 5. There's a fair amount of parking along the street or in the small lot at cove 2.

and walk to the beach. You could also unload your gear quickly near the cove, move your car, and return to gear up. The layout at all three coves makes it easy to gear up at the beach (**Figures 2 and 4**).

Amenities
It's all here (**Figures 5-8**). Bathrooms with changing space, easy shore access, an outdoor shower, and posted site information. And restaurants.

Reef structure
There is a potpourri of structure here, mostly at Cove 2 (the following refers only to Cove 2). One remarkable structure is a maze of old pilings sticking out of the ocean floor at odd angles. On bad viz days these seem to appear out of nowhere and surprise you. Watch closely in front of you. Honey Bear is a sunken 40 foot cabin cruiser just east of the red and white can buoy. There should be a rope leading from the can buoy to Honey Bear (5/08). A set of massive (bent) I-beams extend from about 85-115 feet depth, just beyond the buoy. Don't visit them unless you have advanced training. If something goes wrong at that depth, your friends may read about you in the Seattle Times or PI the next day.

Surface landmarks
The most important landmark at Seacrest is the red and white surface buoy moored near Honey Bear. Yellow buoys have been installed around the water taxi pier (**Figures 5 and 6 and 7**). Rules regarding where not to dive are posted on the pier. Read them (**Figure 8**). Stay outside of the buoys, or you risk being struck by one of the water taxis. Even worse, if we divers break the rules enough times, this place may become off-limits to us.

Swimming to the reef
The best way to enter the water at any of the coves is to walk straight down the beach into the water. At Cove 2 you can see the red and white can buoy anchored near the sunken cabin cruiser (Honey Bear) (**Figure 4**).

Currents
Located deep inside Elliott Bay protects Seacrest from troublesome currents.

bathrooms with changing space

Figure 6. The shower is turned off in winter.

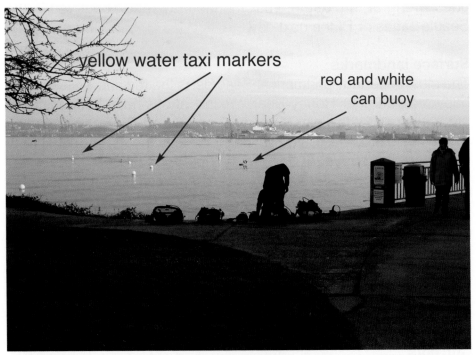

yellow water taxi markers

red and white
can buoy

*Figure 7. Cove 2 is marked for safety. Yellow buoys outline
the no-dive zone to the right of the pier.*

Figure 8. Posted signs show where not to dive. Study them beforehand. This section of rope runs below the yellow marker buoys. But the underwater markers can be tough to follow, and we suspect that it will change over time. You need to be vigilant about where you are and how to avoid the no-dive zone.

Hazards

Discussing the hazards of the Coves is a little complicated. Although there is no official count that we are aware of, it seems that there are more scuba accidents here than at any other dive site in Puget Sound. Despite the accidents that occasionally make the Seattle papers, this is a pretty safe spot as long as you stay away from the water taxi. The currents are relatively mild and the tide level has little effect on dive conditions.

Diver accidents at Seacrest likely relate to the fact that the Coves are such a popular training spot. Think about it—you've got a lot of newbies getting their early dives, and

water taxi

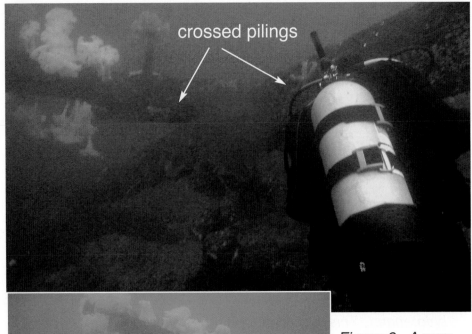

crossed pilings

Figure 9. A number of derelict pilings project from the ocean floor. They make for some eerie scenes, especially in poor visibility conditions. Watch out in front of you as you dive here!

metal tubs, etc.
10-20 feet depth

Figure 10. There is a large variety of metal junk strewn around the ocean floor here.

experienced divers trying out new equipment. Given the large number of divers who use this site, it may be one of the *safer* places, since currents are mild and there are often experienced divers in the vicinity in case of emergency.

You're in trouble when...

Be sure you know where you are in relation to the underwater structure. It is easy to get disoriented here and wind up too near the dock. Also, the bottom drops off rapidly. If you are more than 60 feet down, you'd better have your advanced open water certification card with you.

Marine life

This area is heavily fished, crabbed, kayaked and dived. The bigger fish generally stay away, but you'll see crustaceans, plumose anemones, smaller fish and seals. And maybe an octo or six gill shark. Especially at night.

Honey Bear deck and bow
35-45 feet depth

Honey Bear deck
35-45 feet depth

Figure 11. The Honey Bear is one of the most accessible ship wrecks for Seattle shore divers.

Figure 12. This giant Pacific octopus was living under the bow of Honey Bear in Sept, 2008.

This mishmash of fallen pilings lies a few feet in front of the Honey Bear bow.

clown dorid (nudibranch)
35-45 feet depth

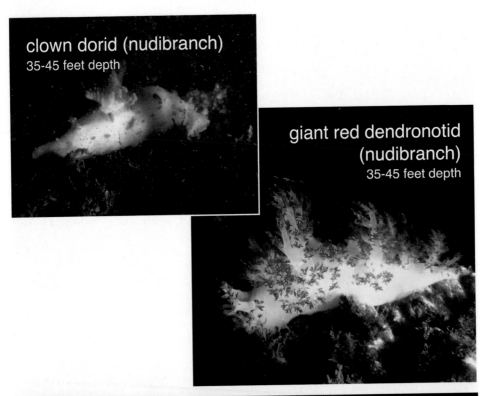

giant red dendronotid (nudibranch)
35-45 feet depth

bent I-beam covered by anemones
85-115 feet depth

orange sea cucumber
4-14 feet depth

kelp crab
20-30 feet depth

clam (piddock)
20-30 feet depth

Salty's on Alki
high-end seafood
1936 Harbor Ave. SW
206 937 1600

Alki Crab and Fish Company
very good, few frills seafood
1660 Harbor Ave. SW
206 938 0975

Some ways that the Seacrest dive sites may change by the time you read this

This is a city-sanctioned dive site. There is some interest in the dive community to make substantial improvements to the reef structure, especially at Cove 1. However, we are unaware of specific plans at this time.

Three Tree Point

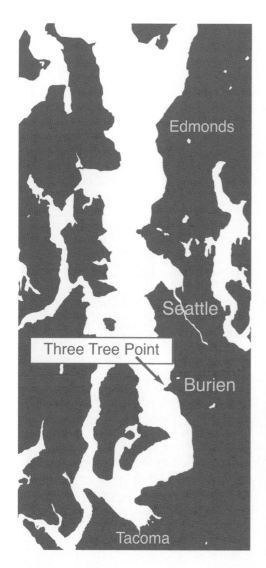

Burien

T hree Tree Point is a popular, unofficial dive spot in which a potpourri of junk has been placed at 30-80 feet depth parallel to the beach. This a bare-bones site. There are no facilities. No bathrooms. No showers. No good place to gear up, other than the back of your car. No nearby restaurants.

In addition to all the amenities that are *not* here, keep in mind that the shoreline on either side of the narrow strip of public access land is privately owned. Respect adjacent property owners. Do not obstruct their driveways. Do not swim ashore on private property.

Figure 1. Three Tree Point is in Burien.

Three Tree Point

Maplewild Ave SW

172nd St SW

170th Pl

the reef structure ("junk") follows the shoreline

60-70 feet depth

30-40 feet depth

Figure 2. Aerial view of the Three Tree Point dive site. (Photo from the Washington State Department of Ecology)

Wait a minute—we don't want to be too negative here. Three Tree is an easy place to start your shore diving experience. It is fairly accessible, and has some amusing structures that are not too difficult to find.

Getting there
Three Tree dive site is on the west side of Puget Sound, about 4 miles south of Seattle. The route there is a little twisty, and you need to look closely at your map. Take exit 154A from I-5 and go east on Route 518. It will turn into SW 148th Street in Burien. Continue on 148th until you get to Ambaum. Take a right at 152nd St NW and go west. 152nd will turn into Maplewild Ave SW, which will wind down to 170th SW. Turn right and you will see the small parking lot ahead. (**Figure 1**).

Parking
Parking is convenient, but limited. There are six spots in a small lot at the top of a short walk leading down to the beach (**Figure 3**). Parking on the adjacent side streets is doable, but tight (**Figure 4**). Be respectful to nearby homeowners.

Amenities
Nada.

Reef Structure
Miscellaneous junk. Sections of pipe, tires, a stove, and bathroom fixtures. One small dinghy, off its trailer. Don't tell Washington Fish and Game about this place.

Surface landmarks
You should see a line of white buoys about 50 yards from shore, at a depth of approximately 55-65 feet depth. Stay inside the buoys. Beyond them, the bottom drops quickly, and there may be small boat traffic overhead.

Swimming to the reef
Gear up at your car and walk down the path to the beach (**Figures 5 and 6**). Carrying stuff to the beach to gear up is difficult because of the steep path and limited beach front.

path to beach

Figure 3. View of the 6-spot parking lot and the beginning of the pathway to the beach.

Figure 4. This view is looking up one of the side streets from the parking lot. If you are here on a sunny weekend, you may have to park your car on one of the narrow side streets.

Figure 5. This is the view looking down from the top of the pathway to beach.

Figure 6. This is the view looking back up to the parking lot. This is a steep climb, that can be difficult if you are fully geared up and emerging from a long dive.

The bottom drops off very quickly—you can be 100 feet down before you know it! It is a surprisingly short swim to the structures. Surface swimming is not necessary. There is a series of white buoys moored at about 55-65 feet depth (**Figure 9**).

We usually submerge as we walk out from the beach, until we find some of the structures. Head north at one depth and back south a little deeper or shallower. You will see reef structure between 30 and 70 feet depth as you head north along the coast.

Currents

Three Tree Point juts out into the Sound, forming a headlands. It intereferes with current flow, setting up lesser eddy currents north and south of the Point. While somewhat unpredictable, the shore structure generally protects this site from stronger currents.

> # Important
>
> There is a continual problem with some nearby property owners and divers regarding scuba parking, trash, noise and trespassing. Most would argue that divers have as much right to use this waterfront as anyone, but we have to be more considerate, or risk having the city move to curtail our use.

Hazards

This site is not an official dive site or marine protected area. Watch out for boats. A dive flag is a good idea. Start back to shore with enough air that you can swim back along the bottom, avoiding boats, currents, and private property.

You know you're in trouble when...

The ocean floor is very steep here. If you are more than 80 feet down, move back towards shore.

Marine life

The area is heavily fished. You'll see mostly crustaceans and small fish. Lots of sea cucumbers and sole. Take time to look in the eel grass at the shallower depths.

Figure 7. Looking northward up the beach. The reef structure runs parallel to the beach, northward.

Figure 8. Looking southward down the beach. Stay off the beaches in front of the private homes that line the adjacent shore.

private homes

white buoys

Figure 9. This is the view from beach. The buoys are anchored to blocks at about 55 feet depth MLLW.

Figure 12. Mother seals leave their pups on shore while they look for food.
Resist the temptation to investigate a beached pup. Keep your distance and do not touch. This diver is too close!

Figure 11. These photos are a sampling of the junk that you'll see here. It's not elegant.

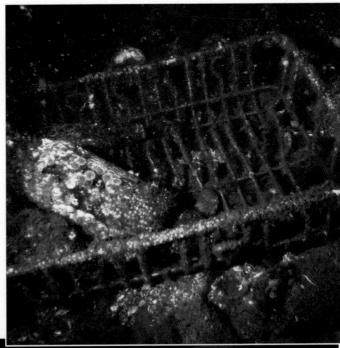

Dungeness crab
30-40 feet depth

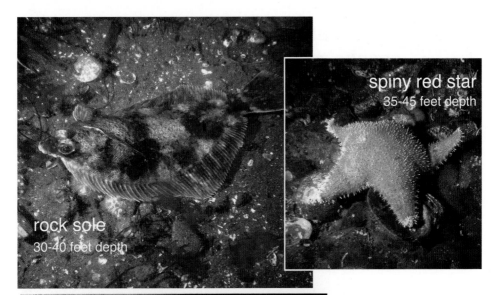

rock sole
30-40 feet depth

spiny red star
35-45 feet depth

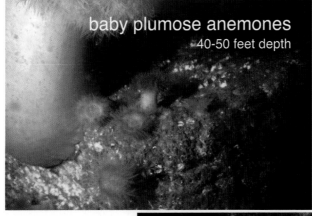

baby plumose anemones
40-50 feet depth

squid eggs
35-45 feet depth

California sea cucumber

> ## Some ways that the Three Tree dive site may change by the time you read this
>
> This is an unofficial dive site with minimal maintenance. Changes to the reef structures occur sporadically, infrequently and unpredictably.

Titlow Marine Park

Tacoma

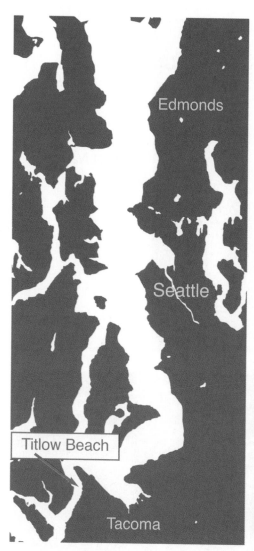

Edmonds

Seattle

Titlow Beach

Tacoma

Titlow Beach, a marine sanctuary, is part of the 58-acre Titlow Park. Attorney Aaron Titlow ran a resort hotel here in the early 1900s. The main reef structures are the remains of a burned out ferry terminal. The extensive pilings, fast currents, and a fishing ban make for a wealth of marine life. This is as close as you can come to diving in a well-stocked aquarium.

The only real problem with this dive site is the same thing responsible for its phenomenal variety of marine life: wicked currents. The strong and somewhat unpredictable currents here requires that you carefully

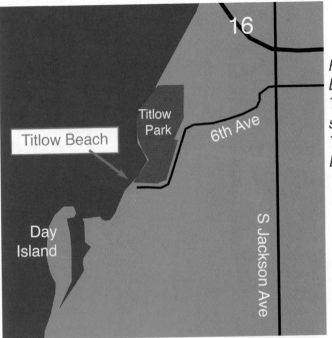

Figure 1. Titlow Beach is in Tacoma, half a mile south of the Tacoma Narrows Bridge.

Figure 2. Aerial view of Titlow Marine Preserve. (Photo from the Washington State Department of Ecology)

plan your dive around slack (or work out with the US Olympic swim team ahead of time).

Getting there

Titlow dive site is a half mile south of the Tacoma Narrows Bridge. Take exit 132 from I-5, onto Route 16 West. Follow 16W to Jackson Ave, the last exit before the Tacoma Narrows Bridge. Go 0.4 miles south on Jackson to 6th Ave and turn west. Follow 6th Ave down to Titlow Park. You will pass a large pool on your right and continue to the observation deck at the waterfront (**Figure 1**).

Parking

Parking is fairly convenient, provided you don't go on a weekend afternoon. There is a row of spots on 6th Ave, just before you get to the waterfront. If you go on a busy weekend, you may have to park in one of the further lots or sidestreets. Don't use the restaurant parking spots adjacent to the observation deck.

We like to pull up to the observation deck, unload our gear quickly and then move our car to one of the lots. Or you can gear up at your car and walk to the observation deck.

Amenities

This place has it all. Showers on site. Picnic tables. Bathrooms in the adjacent parkland. Steamers restaurant serves good quality seafood and has comfortable seating—a good place to rest and trade stories.

Reef Structure

The pilings. They're covered with life, and there is an abundance of life on the ocean floor nearby. There are boulders and ledgers to the south and west, but venturing out of sight of the ferry pilings should be left for experienced divers. Depth at the bottom of the pilings ranges from about 15-25 feet depth.

Surface landmarks

The pilings.

Figure 3. The burned-out ferry dock at Titlow is a wildlife marvel, above and below water. Unfortunately, the state is planning to remove the pilings due to their creosote treatment

Swimming to the reef

Walk down the beach path (**Figure 6**) and swim out between rows of short pilings (**Figure 11**). Even here, use you compass to make sure you stay on course. Go to the surface to check along the way, if unsure. Once you get to the ferry dock pilings, make a circle around them, both inside and outside, if your air supply permits.

Currents

Very strong. This place is more dangerous than any other dive site described in this book. You absolutely must plan your dive to avoid high flow times.

Hazards

Strong currents. Sorry, we said it again. There is boat traffic beyond the pilings (where you should not go).

Your know you're in trouble when...

If you cannot see at least one of the pilings at all times, get concerned immediately. Be sure you know where you are and that you have enough air to return along the bottom. If you get lost, surface carefully to check your bearings or head back in the direction towards shore, along the bottom.

Marine life

Awesome. Especially the anemone-laden pilings. Mostly smaller fish. Giant barnacles love the currents here.

Tacoma Narrows bridge

Figure 4. Looking north, you can see the Tacoma Narrows bridge from the observation deck .

Figure 5. Looking south from the beach, you can see Day Island. An underwater wall off Day Island is a popular boat dive.

Day Island

observation deck

shower

stairs down to water

Figure 6. This drop-off spot on the observation deck can be used to unload gear. Unload quickly and move your car to one of the lots.

Figure 7. There is a long row of parking spots just south of the observation deck.

observation deck

row of parking spots

244

Figure 8. The observation deck, with tables, is a popular picnic spot for non-divers. Although many non-divers want to talk about "what's out there", others don't want dripping wet suits near their tables. Be considerate.

high tide

low tide

Figure 9. View from beach at high versus low tide. We prefer to dive here at high tide. Especially during high plankton times.

245

Figure 10. View from beach at high tide. Swim out between the pilings, but keep a compass reading to double check that you stay on course.

Figure 11. We're not kidding about the current here! This is how the bull kelp looks at any time other than slack.

hallway
through
pilings
18-28 feet depth

large sun stars

Figure 12. This dive site is mostly about the pilings from the old ferry dock. There is a stunning array of anemones. It is downright fun to swim among the pilings along the ocean floor.

fallen piling
16-26 feet depth

lingcod
19-29 feet depth

giant barnacles
20-30 feet depth

leather star
20-30 feet depth

cabezon
(marbled sculpin)
18-28 feet depth

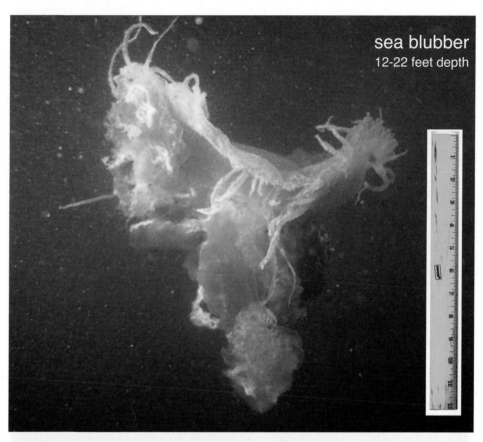

sea blubber
12-22 feet depth

wolf eel
21-22 feet depth

Steamer's
casual seafood

8802 6th Ave
253 565 4532

Beach Tavern
casual food and beer

8612 6th Ave
253 564 9984

Some ways that the Titlow dive site may change by the time you read this

This is a city-sanctioned dive site. Major changes are being planned, including removal of the creosote-treated pilings, and placement of an extensive artificial reef. These changes may occur in 2010.

The future of shore diving

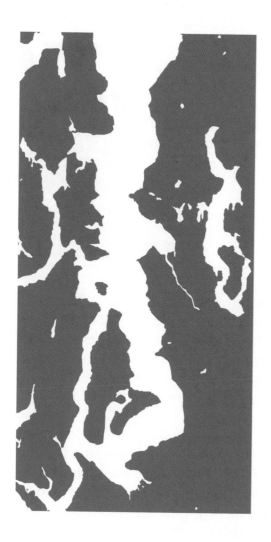

The eleven dive sites described in this book are the most popular ones within a 30 minute drive from downtown Seattle. They range from bare bones (Three Tree Point) to scuba heaven (Bruce Higgins Underwater Trails). Considering the population pressure on the Sound, we believe that shore diving in the urban area around Seattle is pretty good. But it could be much better. And it could be a lot worse.

Even in the two years it took to put this book together, there have been many minor and some major dive site changes. The most dramatic will be the removal of the oil dock at Edmonds Marina Beach. The dock is to be removed, in part, to get rid of creosote-soaked pil-

People For Puget Sound, established in 1991, is a citizens group educating and advocating for protection and restoration of the Sound. Although not a dive organization, People For Puget Sound shares a mission that meshes with diving interests.

To donate:
www.pugetsound.org
or
206 382 7007

PEOPLE

F O R

PUGET

SOUND

ings, which are now considered an environmental hazard. The same issue is likely to result in the removal of the old ferry dock at Titlow Marine Preserve. These pilings have long been a prime dive attraction, serving as home for a large variety of marine life. We will mourn the loss of the Marina Beach oil dock, and many divers will likely go into a severe depression when the Titlow pilings are taken. But such is the future.

Instead of going depressed, we recommend that divers step forward to help make those changes positive. Otherwise, we will face a future with fewer and fewer shore dive options. The alternative is to be left with boat dives, which require money, gas, and more time. Enhancing shore dive sites will keep scuba diving accessible and affordable to us masses.

The ideal shore dive site has easy shore access and interesting underwater structure. A nearby bathroom, change room, and shower are nice, but not essential. Of the sites described in this book, only three have it all. We wish that there were more really good shore dive sites around Puget Sound. More and improved dive sites will foster a closer relationship between citizens and the water around us. More scuba means more advocates for a healthy Sound.

Improving any Puget Sound shore dive site is a bureaucratic challenge. Doing things properly requires approval from a variety of governmental agencies, some of which have conflicting objectives.

There is no official governmental scuba agency to push the process. What we really need is a scuba-crazed governor to push hard for scuba political action. If you can't run for governor, there still are ways to help. Donate. Join. Volunteer.

The most influential general interest organization is People For Puget Sound. These people are working to make a better existence for us. Help them do it. Money matters. Considering how much dinero we divers spend on equipment, sending a couple of $50 or $100 checks to such organizations is a relatively small sacrifice to help them enhance our scuba lives.

Regional dive clubs also spend considerable effort maintaining dive sites. They include the Marker Buoys, Moss Bay Dive Club, Puget Sound Depth Chargers, Emerald Sea Dive Club and the Boeing Seahorses. Join one or more. The more people join, the more clout we will have to protect the Sound and enhance scuba sites.

Donate. Join. Volunteer.

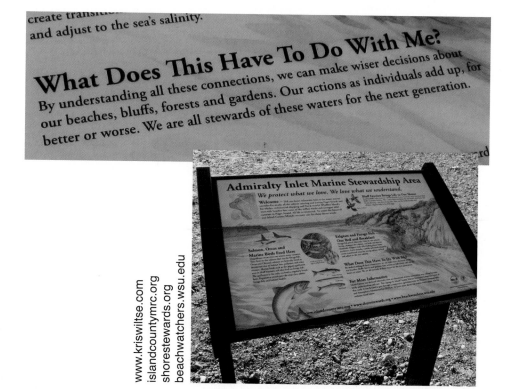

www.kriswiltse.com
islandcountymrc.org
shorestewards.org
beachwatchers.wsu.edu

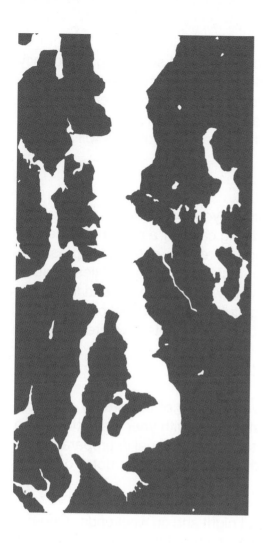

A few more things...

W e expect that a wide variety of people will read through this book. Some will be potential divers, trying to decide whether to *take the plunge*. Others will will be heavily seasoned. And some never-to-be divers may look through it simply because they are curious about *what's down there*. There will likely be some divers from other places who are considering coming to Puget Sound to try cold water diving. There will also be some parents whose children express an interest in starting to dive. We'd like to add a few points in these various regards.

What it takes physically

Diving safely requires a reasonable degree of swimming proficiency and physical fitness. You don't need to be a cross between Arnold, Serena and Lance, but you should be able to swim several pool laps comfortably (200 yards) without having to lie down and suck pure oxygen afterwards. A history of heart or inner ear problems will likely require a physician's clearance.

What it takes mentally

Safe diving requires a commitment on your part to learn and practice proper technique. Beyond that, diving calls for a reasonable degree of concentration and determination to remain cool under pressure. You don't have to be a James Bond clone. These qualities exist, or can be cultivated, in most people who would bother to read this book. Remember, most of the interesting stuff is within 40 feet of the surface of Puget Sound. You don't need to push the limits to where no person has gone before.

Getting certified

Certification classes require several hours of classroom and pool time, and four one-hour open water dives with your instructor. Plan to spend several hours studying technical material in preparation for the classes. The open water dives are generally done over the course of two half-days.

Group classes are mostly offered at night and on weekends. One-on-one instruction is widely available. Instructional fees are typically $200-400.

What it costs

It's not cheap. Certification lessons run about $300. A complete set of equipment ranges from $1,200 to $2,500. Each tank fill costs about $6. Assuming you start from scratch to get certified, equipped and dive 20 times in a year, your first year's costs would be approximately $1,500 (**Figure 1**). Diving costs are roughly on par with downhill skiing, but higher than hiking or bicycling.

If you are new to Puget Sound diving, it is not a bad idea to rent equipment for your first couple of dives to make sure you really want to pursue this. We did so, and went on to be scuba-nuts. But you

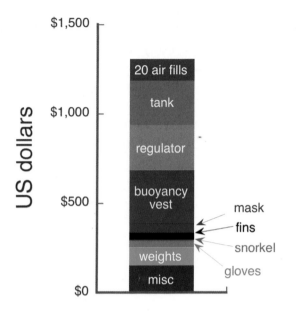

Figure 1. The cost to purchase equipment and make 20 dives in a year runs approximately $1,500, excluding transportation.

should not assume that this is really for you until you've been under a few times. Renting equipment for a day or two will put you back about $100.

Kids

Scuba diving can be a great family activity—many divers get started with a parent. Diving can bring out the best in young people—they typically understand that this is serious, and tend to act accordingly. Kids who don't take diving seriously should not do it. Although some parents might consider diving too risky for kids, others will see the challenge as a plus.

Letting kids dive without an adult is like letting kids see R-rated movies—there is a wide range of what parents find acceptable. We have reluctantly allowed our highly experienced 16 year-old to dive with friends, without an adult present.

Traveling here to dive

We'd love to see more people from Puget Sound and elsewhere discover diving here. The state of Washington would also like to see

259

more divers, partly because it is a form of tourism (translation: *more revenue*). If you are thinking of making a trip here to try it, we advise careful consideraton of your travel plans. Unlike tropical diving, the conditions here can be highly variable from day-to-day. So picking a couple of days far in advance and making expensive travel plans could be problematic. Give some thought to the time of year you come. Review Chapter 4 carefully. And whatever time you choose, it is better to plan on being here for a few days with other things to do, in case you need to wait a day or two for better conditions.